STUDIES ON ISTANBUL AND BEYOND

★

View of the Golden Horn, looking to the northeast from the area of the Fatih Camii.

(Postcard, from the collection of Nezih Başgelen, Istanbul, produced by the Neue Photographische Gesellschaft A.G. Berlin-Steglitz, 1907.)

STUDIES ON ISTANBUL AND BEYOND

THE FREELY PAPERS · VOLUME I

Edited by

ROBERT G. OUSTERHOUT

UNIVERSITY OF PENNSYLVANIA

Museum of Archaeology and Anthropology

PHILADELPHIA

LIBRARY OF CONGRESS CATALOGING IN PUBLICATION DATA

Studies on Istanbul and beyond / edited by Robert G. Ousterhout. -- 1st ed.
    p. cm.
    Includes bibliographical references and index.
    ISBN 978-1-934536-01-8 (hardcover : alk. paper) 1. Istanbul (Turkey)--
History. 2. Turkey--History--Ottoman Empire, 1288-1918. I. Ousterhout,
Robert G.
    DR728.S78 2007
    949.61'8015--dc22

                                                        2007033780

ISBN 10: 1-934536-01-6
ISBN 13: 978-1-934536-01-8

*Published with the assistance of
the Joukowsky Family Foundation and the
American Research Institute in Turkey*

FOREWORD

NINA J. KÖPRÜLÜ

This collection of work by the John Freely Fellows, initiated and sponsored by the Joukowsky Family Foundation and awarded annually through the American Research Institute in Turkey (ARIT), is a celebration of John Freely's lifelong passion for and curiosity about Istanbul, Turkey. The fellowship was envisioned to cultivate research about the city, its history, and its institutions by supporting graduate and post-doctoral scholars through their fieldwork and archival investigations.

Since 2001 the Joukowsky Family Foundation (as sponsor) and ARIT (as manager) have developed a collaborative approach to identifying talented scholars. The John Freely Fellowship is emblematic of the Foundation's broad support for primary research in the region as well as interests in regularly sponsoring the preservation of archaeological sites and architectural monuments. The Foundation recognizes and applauds the unparalleled opportunities organizations such as ARIT offer for research and scholarly experiences *in situ*.

The publication of this volume is also made possible by editor Robert G. Ousterhout, a close friend and admirer of John Freely's, whose dedication to Istanbul is matched only by that of Freely himself. The Foundation is grateful for Professor Ousterhout's commitment to bringing this project to fruition. Additional thanks for general oversight of the publication go to Mark Donovan.

The Foundation congratulates the contributors to this volume and hopes that it will continue to foster, just as John Freely does, affection and interest in Istanbul.

CONTENTS

INTRODUCTION

ROBERT G. OUSTERHOUT

This city grabs you by the heart and never lets you go.
John Freely on Istanbul

In September 1960 John Freely and his family stepped off an airplane at Yeşilköy Airport in Istanbul, and it was love at first sight. Those who know John Freely might argue that there was a well-developed predisposition to fall in love with the city, while others maintain that it was quite simply his destiny. Having left behind the security of a research position at Princeton, Freely had jumped ship in search of adventure, accepting a teaching position, sight unseen, on the Physics faculty at what was then Robert College (now Boğaziçi University). For John, his wife Dolores, and children Maureen, Brendan, and Eileen, Istanbul became the adventure of a lifetime, punctuated in the early days by mandatory family treks through the Old City every Saturday.

It was the perfect time to be in Istanbul. The population was a fraction of what it is today; the Marmara's waters were still clean enough to swim in; urban redevelopment was at best limited in scope—the age of grand planning schemes had yet to begin. Modernism, signaled by the opening of the Hilton Hotel in 1955, was the dream of many, but the city clung stubbornly to its past, with mosques and minarets defiantly dominating the skyline. Moreover, large areas of the Old City still lay bare from the fires of the early 20th century, and the palimpsest of history was everywhere visible. The Walker Trust had finished its second round of excavations on the site of the Great Palace; the Byzantine Institute of America and the Dumbarton Oaks Field Committee had only recently completed their cleaning and consolidation of the mosaics at the Ayasofya and at the Kariye Camii, and the latter organization had expanded its investigations into the Fethiye Camii, the Zeyrek Camii, the Saraçhane, and elsewhere. It was a time of discovery, although international interest and large-scale tourism had yet to develop—Melina Mercouri did not make the film *Topkapi* until 1964.

In short, the city became the Freelys' playground.

Although trained as a physicist, Freely, Irish by descent, spent part of his childhood in Ireland; storytelling is in his blood. Perhaps it all began with a story. Freely's great-grandfather served in the British army and fought in the Crimean

War when he was 17 years old. "He was wounded in the last battle of the war and treated at the Florence Nightingale Hospital in Istanbul in 1856," Freely relates. "The stories he told about the war were passed on to me by my mother and grandmother, so I first heard about the city when I was five years old."

A good tale is worth retelling, expanding, and elaborating. The adventure of Istanbul, with its rich layering of history, demanded a narrative, and in 1966 Freely began to write it. When he discovered that his Robert College colleague Hilary Sumner-Boyd had been doing the same, focusing on the antiquities of the city, the two joined forces to produce *Strolling through Istanbul*, which was first published in 1972 by Redhouse Press (Istanbul). Since that time, the book has gone through countless reprintings and is still in print. It remains the best guidebook ever written about Istanbul, setting a standard for travel writing that is rarely matched. Effortlessly combining the physicist's eye for detail with the Irish love of a good tale, the book is punctuated with exclamation points that reveal the writer's enthusiasm for his subject, and insightful personal observations lead the reader step by step through the streets and alleys of the city and deep into its colorful past. The imaret at the Lâleli Cami, for example, is said to be "an attractive little building with a very strange plan indeed, quite impossible to describe: it must be inspected." The mosque itself has "amusing but pointless galleries." Elsewhere the reader is instructed to relax in a teahouse "under the shade of that giant çinar which a poet once called the Tree of Idleness." How could one *not* be taken in by such descriptions as these?

Strolling through Istanbul opened the floodgates, as Freely found his true calling. Although he continued to work as a physicist, he went on to write more than 40 books in his spare time. He became one of the best-known travel writers internationally, with books devoted to Athens, the Greek Islands, Crete, Boston, Venice, and the different regions of Turkey. But Istanbul remained his spiritual home, a city to which he kept returning, living there 1960–76, 1988–91, and from 1995 onward. Istanbul was the ultimate adventure, and time and time again, Freely the writer returned to investigate its monuments and its rich history, finding an expanding audience of readers with each new book—on diverse subjects ranging from Byzantine churches to lost messiahs, from the Seraglio to the architect Sinan.

Editing this volume has been a labor of love, as I've known John Freely for years. We both love Istanbul, and we both love a good adventure. We even like bad adventures. He'll call me, excited to share a new discovery, and then we'll head off into the Old City, only to get completely lost in the process. Since I met John, "strolling through Istanbul" has taken on an entirely new meaning. We never seem to find what we're looking for, but we usually have quite a good time in the process. I'll struggle gamely with interpreting John's muddled directions into street Turkish, while he regales whomever is listening with an amusing story his Irish grandmother once told him. We thus meet a variety of eccentric locals in the process, and once we're worn out (John) and exasperated (me), we'll find a perfectly disreputable place to eat lunch. One of our repeatable and often repeated discussions on the identification and chronology of Byzantine and Ottoman monuments has been shorthanded over the years to: Question—"Is Byz?" Reply—"Not. Ott." We've done this routine often enough that none but the two of us finds it amusing.

In July 2006, John Freely celebrated his 80th birthday surrounded by family, friends, colleagues, and devoted admirers. The gala, all-day event was hosted by Boğaziçi University, an institution with which Freely has been associated throughout much of his career, but more importantly, the event took place in a city that has become almost synonymous with his name. Freely has introduced Istanbul to countless readers—serious travelers, armchair adventurers, and scholars alike. In fact, it is hard to speak of Istanbul without mentioning John Freely, for many of us first saw the city through his eyes or first imagined the city through his words.

This close association of the man and the city motivated his friend and fellow Istanbul-lover Nina Joukowsky Köprülü to establish a fellowship in his name, the John Freely Fellowship, which is awarded annually through the American Research Institute in Turkey. First offered in 2001, the Freely Fellowships have supported nine scholars to date, and the chapters included in this volume represent its first fruits.

John Freely at his 80th birthday party, flanked by Nina J. Köprülü and Robert G. Ousterhout (July 2006).

Şehname of Selim II (Topkapı Library, Istanbul, ms. no. A 3595, folio 13a): The Court Historian Seyyid Lokman and Grand Vizier Sokollu Mehmed Paşa in Audience with Selim II (courtesy of Topkapı Library).

THE OFFICE OF THE OTTOMAN COURT HISTORIAN

EMINE FETVACİ

The illustrated manuscripts produced by the office of the Ottoman court historian (*şehnameci*) during the last quarter of the 16th century were instrumental in negotiating the changing social hierarchies of the Ottoman court during the same period. Ottoman *şehname*s commented on contemporary events, promoted the political agendas of courtiers as well as the sultan, and helped characterize their patrons and creators in highly nuanced ways. Neither passive ornaments nor formulaic eulogies of the sultan, these texts exerted significant agency in shaping the perspectives of their elite audiences in the Ottoman palace. They were of central importance for shaping history itself.

Any attempt to analyze these influential books must take into account their author, the *şehnameci*. Christine Woodhead's seminal study, "An Experiment in Official Historiography: The Post of Şehnāmeci in the Ottoman Empire, c. 1555–1605," has defined our understanding of the official court historian for many years. [1] Woodhead identified the *şehnameci*'s main responsibility as "compos[ing] literary accounts of contemporary or near-contemporary Ottoman history," and described their contents as flattering the ruler and having eulogistic overtones. [2] She characterized the position as a "permanent and salaried" post established by Sultan Süleyman in the 1550s but that disappeared after 1605. Woodhead rightfully pointed to the *Shahnama* of Firdawsi as a conceptual model for the Ottoman *şehname*. [3] Her study reviewed the careers of all five people who held the position during its 50 years of existence and summarized their work in an effort to define the nature of the position.

[1] Christine Woodhead, "An Experiment in Official Historiography: The Post of Şehnāmeci in the Ottoman Empire, c. 1555–1605," *Wiener Zeitschrift für die Kunde des Morgenlandes* 75 (1983): 157–82. Bekir Kütükoğlu, "Şehnâmeci Lokman," in N. Kütükoğlu, ed., *Prof. Dr. Bekir Kütükoğlu'na Armağan* (Istanbul: Edebiyat Fakültesi Basımevi, 1991), 39–48, originally a paper delivered at the Third Seminar on Art Historical Research in Istanbul in 1982, has similarly been very influential but is less comprehensive than Woodhead, being a study of the career of a single historian rather than an attempt to define the office.

[2] Woodhead, "Experiment," 157, 159.　　　　[3] Ibid., 158–59.

This chapter re-evaluates the office of the *şehnameci* based on a close reading of archival documents relating to the *şehnameci* Seyyid Lokman and the contents of his *şehname*s. Such a juxtaposition brings to light important nuances about Lokman's career that have thus far escaped our attention. Lokman was the *şehnameci* from 1569 until 1596–97—in other words, for much of the existence the office. He was also the most prolific among his colleagues, composing ten of the fifteen works produced by Ottoman *şehnameci*s.[4] In theory, our understanding of the role fulfilled by the *şehnameci* should accord with the realities of Lokman's life more than any other holder of this office. Yet, when we examine Lokman's biography—as evinced by the archival documents—in tandem with his production—as seen in the *şehname*s—the discrepancies between our conception of the position and Lokman's realities become clear.

The documents in question—mostly from the Prime Ministry Archives in Istanbul—demonstrate the extent of Lokman's duties and responsibilities, revealing that his position was as much an administrative as a creative one.[5] He was clearly responsible for all aspects of production, from composing the text to choosing a team of artists and scribes, overseeing their salaries, and even acquiring the necessary materials, such as paper. Secondly, and perhaps more importantly, Lokman's position was not nearly as "permanent" as we have imagined it to be. The contents of some of the manuscripts Lokman composed, examined later in this chapter, clearly support this reading and indicate the more occasional nature of his work.

The administrative aspects of Lokman's work come to the fore in a very pronounced fashion through the documents. Lokman was in charge of gathering materials, supervising scribes, painters, binders, illuminators, and others who worked on the creation of the books. While this is not a new piece of information, it has not been taken into account by historians seeking to define the nature of the office of the *şehnameci* or by those analyzing the books composed by Lokman. Art historians have tended to assign creative responsibility to the painters listed on these documents rather than to the *şehnameci* who supervised them. The documents listing those working under Lokman's guidance have been used primarily to identify the names of specific artists working on each of Lokman's books.[6]

---

[4] Ibid.

[5] The documents cited here are all from the Prime Ministry Archives in Istanbul and come from the Kamil Kepeci records; thus the register numbers are KK register no., page no. (KK 252, p. 163).

[6] A select few publications include Nigar Anafarta, *Hünername: Minyatürleri ve Sanatçıları* (Istanbul: Doğan Kardeş Yayınları, 1969); Filiz Çağman, "Şehname-i Selim Han ve Miny-

In his role as administrator Lokman clearly took responsibility for the compensation of those who worked under his direction. He submitted numerous petitions to have the salary of a deceased artist or scribe transferred to one still working or employed in their stead.[7] He also appears to have defended his team and requested raises for them when they had been overlooked: Molla Kasım, for example, who worked on the *Zübdetü't-Tevarih* and the *Surname*, clearly did not receive a sufficient raise in Lokman's eyes, so he asked for him to get an extra five aspers in recognition of his scribal work on the *Surname*.[8] With each manuscript presented to the court the artisans under Lokman's supervision received extra compensation for their work as well as higher appointments. Lokman recorded these salaries in his notebook, indicating once again that he was responsible for them.[9] As did many Ottoman government officials of the time, Lokman looked out for his family members as his own fortunes improved. We learn from the same documents that his nephew was appointed to the scribal corps in 1584 and that his son joined the elite corps of imperial servants (*müteferrika*) in 1589. Lokman was thus in a position to influence the careers of others.[10]

At times Lokman functioned somewhat like a talent scout, requesting that specific individuals be appointed to his projects. Not only did he bring in someone from the cannonball corps to work on the production of the manuscript of the *Zübdetü't-Tevarih*, but he also asked for one of the royal guards (*silahdaran-ı dergah-ı 'ali*), Hasan Ibrahim, to be employed for the same project and brought in Hüseyin the gold worker for another project specifically because he wanted him to do the gold leaf on the pages.[11] He also included talented scribes in his team whenever he could—he asked for Mehmed, from the gatekeepers' corps, to be appointed as a scribe to the *şehnameci*s because of his

atürleri," *Sanat Tarihi Yıllığı* 5 (1972–73): 411–42; Günsel Renda, "Topkapı Sarayı Müzesindeki H. 1321 no.lu Silsilename'nin Minyatürleri," *Sanat Tarihi Yıllığı* 5 (1972–73): 443–80; Günsel Renda, "Chester Beatty Kitaplığındaki Zübdetü't-Tevarih ve Minyatürleri," in N. Kütükoğlu, ed., *Prof. Dr. Bekir Kütükoğlu'na Armağan* (Istanbul: Edebiyat Fakültesi Basımevi, 1991), 458–506; Nurhan Atasoy, *1582 Surname-i Humayun: An Imperial Celebration* (Istanbul: Koçbank, 1997); Şule Aksoy, "Sultan III. Murad için Hazırlanmış bir Şehname: Zübdetü't-Tevarih," *P: Sanat, Kültür, Antika* 3 (Fall 1996): 17–37. A large number of the documents are listed and transcribed by Hilal Kazan, "Arşiv Belgeleri Işığında Şehnameci Seyyid Lokman'ın Saray İçin Hazırladığı Eserler," forthcoming in *Studies on Islamic Art and Architecture in Honor of Filiz Çağman* (Istanbul: Topkapı Sarayı).

[7] KK 239, p. 129; KK 242, p. 393; KK 246, p. 68.

[8] KK 250, p. 33.

[9] KK 250, p. 37, for example, states that it is from the sealed record book of Lokman, "Şehname-guy Lokman Efendiānin mühürlü defterüdür."

[10] KK 242, p. 10; KK 252, p. 23.   [11] KK 242, pp. 305, 294.

talent.[12] Lokman was clearly as conscientious about the aesthetic properties of the *şehnames* as he was about their content, and therefore any analysis of his position must consider the physical realities and visual aspects of the books. Lokman's requests for paper and other materials through the office of the paper supervisor (*kağıd emini*) or the city prefect (*şehremini*) also point to the administrative aspect of the position and highlight his responsibility for the entire finished product: not just the words of the *şehname*s, but also their entire physical incarnation, with their paper, ink, and bindings, their texts, and their images.[13]

Lokman himself was also asked to oversee the production of books that he had not composed. A document dated 1588 lists the raises received by those who worked on the *Surname* and the *Hünername*, from Lokman's records.[14] The document makes clear that Lokman supervised the production of the *Surname*, a manuscript composed by the scribe İntizami.[15] Lokman was not the only one responsible for overseeing the illustrations of histories at the Ottoman court. We know of at least one other individual: the historian Mustafa Âli was appointed to oversee the creation of a luxurious illustrated version of his own account of the Georgian campaigns of Lala Mustafa Paşa, the *Nusretname*.[16]

In addition to Lokman's administrative responsibilities, the documents indicate that the work of the *şehnameci* was rather occasional in nature. We have thus far imagined him in constant charge of a group of artists and scribes bringing his projects to life, but this consistency seems less clear in light of the archival documentation. A core group of painters (Osman, Ali, Lütfü, and Velican), scribes (Haydar and Sinan), and illuminators (Musa Ahmed) collaborated on a number of projects under Lokman,[17] yet the records refer to these men (among others) as being in the old corps of royal designers (*cemâ'at-i nakkaşân-ı hassa-i kadîmî*), the old corps of royal book scribes (*cemâ'at-i kâtibân-ı kütüb-i kadîm*), or the royal corps of binders (*cemâ'at-i mücellidân-ı hassa*).[18] Their primary affiliations were with established groups within the

---

[12] KK 253, p. 31.

[13] KK 230, p. 319; and Topkapı Palace Archives no. E 2114; both deal with Lokman's request for paper and other supplies.

[14] KK 250, p. 37. Additionally, KK 250, p. 33 records that Lokman asked for a raise for the scribe and artist Molla Kasım for his work on the *Surname*.

[15] For the *Surname* and its author, see also Nurhan Atasoy, *1582 Surname-i Humayun: An Imperial Celebration* (Istanbul: Koçbank, 1997).

[16] Cornell Fleischer, *Bureaucrat and Intellectual in the Ottoman Empire: the Historian Mustafa Âli* (Princeton, NJ: Princeton University Press, 1986), 109–11.

[17] These names were also identified by Çağman, Renda, and others.

[18] KK 242, pp. 10–11; KK 252, pp. 23–24.

royal corps of artisans. That the same artist worked on more than one manuscript with Lokman does not mean that that artist was employed on a permanent basis under the *şehnameci*. It appears, rather, that these men were categorically employed in the corps of artisans (*ehl-i hiref*) and came together under Lokman's guidance for specific projects, probably on an ad-hoc basis.

Many other artisans were hired from the outside on a similar temporary basis, as the project required. Three artists and two scribes were brought in (*etraftan*, from the "vicinity") for the *Zübdetü't-Tevarih*, and they subsequently received positions within the corps of artisans.[19] For example, Velican, who later worked on the *Hünername* and the *Surname*, was one of those brought in for the *Zübdetü't-Tevarih*.[20] Lokman also hired other people who did not continue as artisans; for example, a man named Musa, from the corps of the cannonballers (*topciyan*), was promoted to an outer service position as doorkeeper (*kapıcı*). Others were also promoted from the *Zübdetü't-Tevarih* team to service far away from the palace—two to Van, two to Karaman, and one to Erzurum.[21] Lokman personally asked for very specific appointments for many of those working on the *Hünername*: in addition to various scribal and artisanal (such as the corps of saddle makers) posts for his employees, he requested appointments to the corps of the messengers, armory, cannonballers, and gatekeepers.[22] Thus we see he temporarily employed palace trainees who were then appointed to outer service branches of the empire.

Lokman's team was flexible enough to expand for those projects that needed more people, from the five working on the *Şehname-i Selim Han* to almost 30 on the production of the *Zübdetü't-Tevarih* and the *Hünername* manuscripts.[23] They might retain their artisan or scribe status once the project was completed, but there does not appear to have been a fixed group under Lokman's continuous direction.

Those who worked on Lokman's manuscripts were also employed on other projects. The chief of the corps of artists (*ser bölük*), Lütfü, and another master artist named Bolad Ahmed, for example, were employed in the decoration of the Old Palace and some imperial caiques (skiffs), for which they received

[19] KK 242, pp. 10–11.

[20] Ibid.; these figures brought in "from the vicinity" also point to the presence of known artisans working freelance in the capital.

[21] Ibid.

[22] KK 252, pp. 23, 24.

[23] Even without access to these documents, Woodhead correctly observes that "the number of specialist staff employed in the *şehnameci*'s office presumably varied with the volume of work to be carried out and awaits further investigation" ("Experiment," 161).

additional compensation.[24] Gülru Necipoğlu has shown that some of the heads of the corps of painters served as building supervisors and were sent to places as diverse as Manisa and Mecca to oversee architectural projects. Lütfü himself was sent to Medina to supervise a project between 1586 and 1589.[25] These multiple appointments, borrowing from the artist talent pool, also illustrate the temporary nature of the ṣehnameci's projects.

The ad-hoc nature of the projects also raises questions about the permanence of Lokman's position. Although we know that he was a salaried official, the association of that salary with the title of ṣehnameci is not as clear. While we learn from Woodhead that Lokman's salary was 30,000 aspers when he was first appointed, other archival records show that he was given a 10,000-asper raise at the completion of each job—the Şehname-i Selim Han, the Zübdetü't-Tevarih, and the first volume of the Şehinṣehname—and a 20,000-asper raise for completing the first volume of the Hünername—again a project-based phenomenon, as was the case for most members of the corps of artists.[26] While it appears that between 1569 and 1589 he had almost tripled his income, with the devaluation of the Ottoman asper in 1584–85, his increase in real income was actually much more modest.[27] With regard to purchasing power, Lokman's income in 1589 was only 1.5 times his income 20 years before, in 1569.[28] We know that nominal incomes did not increase at the rate of inflation during this period; thus Lokman appears to have fared better than many of his contemporaries.[29]

The ṣehnameci's membership in the müteferrika confirms that he was a prestigious figure.[30] Lokman's appointment to this elite group was recorded in March 1575, correcting an earlier oversight.[31] Contrary to Woodhead's asser-

---

[24] KK 242, p. 220.

[25] Gülru Necipoğlu, The Age of Sinan: Architectural Culture in the Ottoman Empire (Princeton, NJ: Princeton University Press, 2005), 178.

[26] KK 238, p. 297 for Şehname-i Selim Han; KK 239, p. 197 for Şehinṣehname; KK 242, pp. 1–2, for the Zübdetü't-Tevarih; KK 252, pp. 23–24 for the Hünername.

[27] I would like to thank Professor Şevket Pamuk for his guidance on price indices, inflation, and relative wages during this period. For an overview of Ottoman monetary history, see Şevket Pamuk, "Evolution of the Ottoman Monetary System, 1326–1914," in Halil İnalcık and Donald Quataert, eds., An Economic and Social History of the Ottoman Empire, Volume Two: 1600–1914 (Cambridge: Cambridge University Press, 1994), 947–80.

[28] My calculations are based on a comparative chart of the incomes of construction workers from 1498 to 1922, in which Professor Pamuk has calculated the real and nominal values of wages; see Şevket Pamuk, 500 Years of Prices and Wages in Istanbul and Other Cities (Ankara: State Institute of Statistics, Prime Ministry of Turkey, 2000), 69, table 4.1.

[29] Ibid., xi–xiii, and personal correspondence.

[30] KK 229, p. 22.   [31] Ibid.

tion that Lokman's membership in the *müteferrika* was a novelty, the first *şehnameci* Arifi had also been a member of this elite group. The order explicitly states that Lokman was given the title *müteferrika*, which his predecessor Fethullah (Arifi) had also held. In 1589, Lokman was provided with an additional salary line by being appointed finance director (*defterdar*).[32] Thus the position of *şehnameci* was not the sole source of his livelihood: in his capacities as *müteferrika* and *defterdar*, he was entitled to a certain amount of income.

The occasional nature of the *şehnameci*'s work is shown by the lack of a permanent studio set aside for Lokman. Current understanding of manuscript production for the Ottoman court locates a royal design studio (*hassa nakkaşhanesi*) during the 16th and early 17th centuries just outside the palace grounds.[33] It is also clear from a 1587 document mentioning repairs to the house of the scribe and painter Molla Kasım, located next to a *nakkaşhane* (painting or design studio), that the royal workshop occupied a fixed physical location.[34] What we do not know is whether there was a special studio for Lokman: it does not appear to be so. Some members of the corps of artists had a studio in the first courtyard of the Topkapı Palace where they prepared designs for decorating palace buildings.[35] Filiz Çağman also argued that temporary studios were probably set up in this part of the palace for special projects, and it is possible that *şehname*s were prepared in such temporary locales as these.[36] Gülru Necipoğlu mentioned a residence known as *şehnameci evi* (house of the *şehnameci*) belonging to the architect Sinan. She suggested that this house had

[32] KK 252, p. 23.

[33] Filiz Çağman, "Saray Nakkaşhanesinin Yeri Üzerinde Düşünceler," in *Sanat Tarihinde Doğudan Batıya: Ünsal Yücel Anısına Sempozyum Bildirileri* (Istanbul: Sandoz Kültür Yayınları, 1989), 35–46, discusses the location of the workshop. Alan Fisher and Carol Garrett Fisher, "A Note on the Location of the Royal Ottoman Painting Ateliers," *Muqarnas* 3 (1985): 118–20, suggest that since the detailed description of the Topkapı Palace by Albert Bobovi in the 17th century did not contain a reference to the court painting atelier, there probably was not one in the palace. They propose that the Ottoman manuscripts might have been created in a similar fashion to contemporary Safavid practices, created piecemeal in other locations and collated at a central library.

[34] Ismail Hakkı Uzunçarşılı, Ibrahim Kemal Baybura, and Ülkü Altındağ, *Topkapı Sarayı Müzesi Osmanlı Saray Arşivi Kataloğu: Hükümler—Beratlar, II. Fasikül E 1–12476* (Ankara: Türk Tarih Kurumu Basımevi, 1988), 115, no. 1102, published the transcription of a royal edict ordering the payment of a certain sum to Molla Kasım for repairs to his house located next to the *nakkaşhane*.

[35] Gülru Necipoğlu, *Architecture, Ceremonial and Power: The Topkapi Palace in the Fifteenth and Sixteenth Centuries* (Cambridge, MA: Architectural History Foundation and MIT Press, 1991), 48, and nn. 73–79.

[36] Çağman, "Saray Nakkaşhanesinin Yeri," 35–46.

originally been owned by Arifi, who had added rooms for the calligraphers working on the five-volume illustrated Ottoman history for Sultan Süleyman.[37] But the house of the *şehnameci* no longer belonged to the *şehnameci*: it had been given to the chief royal architect instead—Sinan mentions it in his endowment deed from ca. 1583–85.[38] The lack of a separate permanent location for *şehname* production may well have been related to the occasional nature of Lokman's work.

Through these documents the picture of Ottoman illustrated history production appears closer to the contours of its Safavid counterpart as delineated by Marianna Shreve Simpson.[39] When examined with an open mind toward the position of the *şehnameci*, the archival documents reveal two significant similarities. First, that Lokman played a highly administrative and all-encompassing role in the production of Ottoman illustrated histories, overseeing all aspects of production from composition to presentation. Nevertheless, and this is the second point, he did not have a permanent team in his employ or a permanent physical office or studio. Lokman assembled his teams on a project basis, borrowing their members from their permanent positions as imperial designers, scribes, and artisans.

The occasional nature of Lokman's work becomes even more striking when we compare his career to the chief architect, Sinan. The documents point to some parallels between the position of the court historian and the court architect that merit such a comparison. Just as Sinan was responsible for everything in his buildings—down to the selection of tiles and other decorative details—Lokman too oversaw the painters, illuminators, and binders working on his books. Sinan also appears to have similarly supervised his employees' compensation, as he too is documented petitioning the chief scribe of the Imperial Council for the addition of new members to the corps of architects and for raises for his men.[40] Comparing the wages of Lokman and Sinan reveals that in terms of purchasing power, Sinan's 65 asper-per-day salary in 1553—assuming he was paid every day as were the members of the Janissary corps—was practically equivalent to Lokman's 30,000 aspers in 1569, implying their positions were of similar prestige.[41]

---

[37] Necipoğlu, *Age of Sinan*, 148–49.   [38] Ibid.

[39] Marianna Shreve Simpson, "The Making of Manuscripts and the Workings of the Kitabkhana in Safavid Iran," in Peter M. Lukehart, ed., *The Artist's Workshop* (Washington, DC: National Gallery of Art, 1993), 105–21.

[40] Necipoğlu, *Age of Sinan*, 156.

[41] Ibid. Necipoğlu also contrasts Sinan's income to that of the agha of janissaries who apparently received 500 aspers a day.

We can see another significant parallel in the career paths of these professions. Architects went on campaigns with the military during the early years of their service, in rather similar fashion to the campaign secretaries that accompanied Ottoman military commanders. Accompanying the army appears to have been strategically important, as is evident from the career trajectories of the last two *şehnameci*s, Talikizade and Hasan Hükmi.[42] The one difference is that while after Sinan, the chief architects were appointed as a result of their contacts in the Harem, the *şehnameci*s still owed their positions to viziers of the Imperial Council.[43]

A comparison of the chief architect and the court historian also highlights the vast differences between these two positions and illuminates the more sporadic nature of Lokman's work. The position of chief royal architect came with responsibilities far beyond those of the *şehnameci*, from setting prices for the construction industry to supervising urban design projects that changed the appearance of the Ottoman capital during the second half of the 16th century. While Sinan was at the head of a clearly identified group of architects that formed a separate hierarchy from the royal corps of artisans, Lokman oversaw occasional, unique projects with artists who were grouped under the chief treasurer, and with scribes who were under the jurisdiction of the chief scribe (*re'isü'l-küttab*).[44]

Lokman's *şehname*s themselves provide further proof of the intermittent nature of his projects. Given his responsibilities for the content and appearance of his manuscripts, any discussion of the manuscripts must consider their verbal and visual programs together. The *şehname*s demonstrate that Lokman was not solely the mouthpiece of the dynasty, but instead catered to the shifting groups of power-wielders in the Ottoman court of the late 16th century. This, in turn, relates to his less than permanent position.

Starting with his first imperial commission, the *History of Sultan Süleyman*, and continuing with his chronicles of the reigns of Selim II and Murad III, *Şehname-i Selim Han* and the *Şehinşehname*, Lokman lavishes more praise and

---

[42] For the career of Talikizade, see Christine Woodhead, *Talikizade's Şehname-i Humayun: A History of the Ottoman Campaign into Hungary, 1593–94* (Berlin: Klaus Schwarz Verlag, 1983); and Christine Woodhead, "From Scribe to Litterateur: The Career of a Sixteenth-Century Ottoman Katib," *Bulletin of the British Society for Middle Eastern Studies* 9/1 (1982): 55–74. Hasan Hükmi had been the campaign secretary of Sinan Paşa, which had clearly paved the way for his appointment as *şehnameci*.

[43] For the appointments of chief royal architects after Sinan, see Necipoğlu, *Age of Sinan*, 506–19.

[44] For the organization of the corps of royal artists, see Rıfkı Melül Meriç, *Türk Nakış San'atı Araştırmaları* (Ankara: Ankara Üniversitesi Ilahiyat Fakültesi, 1953), vi–vii.

attention on those around the sultan than on the ruler himself.[45] The *History of Sultan Süleyman* extols the virtues of Süleyman's last grand vizier, Sokollu Mehmed Paşa, who was Lokman's greatest patron and the one who brought him to the position of *şehnameci*. Almost two-thirds of the book relates to the Szigetvàr campaign of 1566, showcasing Sokollu's military skills and his political astuteness in ensuring the smooth transition of power to Selim II (r. 1566–74).[46] Lokman's second project as *şehnameci*, the *Şehname-i Selim Han*, though ostensibly an account of the reign of Selim II, begins with the same emphasis on Sokollu, but its second half celebrates the viziers Sinan Paşa and Lala Mustafa Paşa, two of the most powerful courtiers of the reigns of Selim II and Murad III (r. 1574–95).[47] Lokman's two-volume account of the reign of Murad III, the *Şehinşehname*, also promotes Murad's viziers. Whether for their military skills or for their financial contributions to the circumcision feast of Murad III's son, Prince Mehmed, the emphasis is clearly on the sultan's deputies.[48] When we examine Lokman's output of both image and text, it becomes obvious that the manuscripts are as much about members of the Ottoman court as they are about the sultan. Thus, the former understanding of the *şehnameci* as the eulogizer of the sultan is not quite accurate: Lokman clearly operated on behalf of a wider circle of courtly power-wielders.

A fuller understanding of the Ottoman *şehname* as an account of the court, not only of the sultan, requires a re-conceptualization of its relationship to Firdawsi's *Shahnama*. In its inception the Ottoman version draws heavily from the Persian prototype, particularly in the case of the first product of the office, the *Süleymanname*,[49] written in Persian verse in the *mutaqarib* meter and depicting a militarily active, hunting, feasting ruler, the similarities are obvious

---

[45] Chester Beatty Library, no. 413. For a detailed discussion of the contents of the manuscript, see Emine Fetvacı, "From Viziers to Eunuchs: Transitions in Ottoman Manuscript Patronage, 1566–1617" (Ph.D. dissertation, Harvard University, 2005), 115–21.

[46] The text was a versification of Feridun Ahmed Beg's prose history of the campaign, which strengthens the connection to Sokollu Mehmed Paşa, as that book also promotes the interests of the grand vizier more than that of any other protagonist. For Sokollu's image in Feridun Ahmed's history, *Nüzhetü'l Ahbar der Sefer-i Sigetvar* (Topkapı Palace Library, hereafter TSK, H. 1339), see Gülru Necipoğlu, "A Period of Transition: Portraits of Selim II," in Selmin Kangal, ed., *The Sultan's Portrait: Picturing the House of Osman* (Istanbul: İş Bankası Yayınları, 2000), 202–7, and Fetvacı, "Viziers to Eunuchs," 97–106.

[47] Emine Fetvacı, "The Production of the *Şehnāme-i Selīm Hān*," forthcoming in *Muqarnas* 26 (2009).

[48] Fetvacı, "Viziers to Eunuchs," 225–30.

[49] TSK H. 1517. This fifth and last volume of a comprehensive history by the first *şehnameci* Arifi was completed in 1558.

and certain.[50] But in the works Lokman produced, the parallels decrease with each successive book. Woodhead discussed some of these changes, such as the move away from Persian verse to Ottoman Turkish prose.[51] The changing image of the Ottoman ruler, which accompanied the shift in content from a sultan-centered account to a court-centered one, deserves comment here. In Lokman's works chronicling the reigns of Selim II and Murad III, the sultan is never depicted as physically active. In the few paintings where the sultan appears in the Şehname-i Selim Han he is seated and giving audience. The same lack of physical activity is true of the paintings in the Şehinşehname. Thus, already from the beginning of Lokman's career, the Ottoman sultan was no longer presented as similar to the Shahnama hero.

Appointed during the reign of the first Ottoman sultan not to go to war with his armies (Selim II), Lokman was the most prolific of the Ottoman şehnamecis and produced histories throughout the reign of Murad III, who rarely, if ever, even left the palace.[52] The Ottoman şehname may have begun as a eulogistic account of Ottoman history in the Shahnama style, but most of the surviving şehnames are highly nuanced panegyric histories addressing multiple power-wielders at the Ottoman court. Despite the retention of the word şehname in most of the manuscripts' titles and the continuing use of the term şehnameci or şehnameguy for the holder of the office, the literary/historical product and the role of its author shifted during the second half of the 16th century.

This new understanding of the nature of Lokman's work may help us understand the lapse of the office of the şehnameci. Woodhead has argued that the disappearance of the position in the early years of the 17th century was due to the increasing impossibility of portraying the Ottoman sultan as a war hero.[53] As demonstrated above, this change was not a development of the 17th century. Already at the beginning of Seyyid Lokman's career, his sultan had ceased going to war, yet he continued to produce şehnames for 30 more years, and subsequently two other şehnamecis were appointed to succeed him. We must seek other explanations for the disappearance of the office in the early

---

[50] The more official character of the Süleymanname and how it contrasts with the intimate depiction of Shahnama heroes was discussed by Gülru Necipoğlu, "A Kānūn for the State, a Canon for the Arts: Conceptualizing the Classical Synthesis of Ottoman Art and Architecture," in Gilles Veinstein, ed., Soliman le magnifique et son temps (Paris: Documentation Française, 1992), 195–216.

[51] Woodhead, "Experiment," 164–67.

[52] Of the 15 works produced by the holders of this office, as Woodhead also points out, 10 were by Lokman; see ibid., "Experiment," 163–64.

[53] Ibid., 181.

17th century. One possible cause may be the increasing factionalization of the Ottoman court at the end of the 16th century and the growing impossibility of having a single official voice for the court.[54] Another explanation may be the broader loss of interest in illustrated manuscripts, a subject requiring further inquiry.

Redefining the role of the *şehnameci* as a man at the service of a wider circle than just the ruler helps explain Lokman's attempts to secure the patronage of various courtiers. This, in turn, may relate to the occasional nature of his work as seen in the archival documents. If his position had been a permanent one, or if he had been solely at the service of the sultan, he would not have felt the need to address or to eulogize other potential patrons. Lokman's prominence was closely connected to the position of his main patron in the Ottoman court, Sokollu Mehmed Paşa, and Sokollu's death in 1579 was of significant consequence for the future of the office of *şehnameci*. After Sokollu's death Lokman tried to gain the patronage of several other Ottoman courtiers, including Murad III's tutor, Hoca Sadeddin, and the grand viziers Siyavuş Paşa and Sinan Paşa.

Lokman's most concerted attempts at securing a patron were directed to Koca Sinan Paşa.[55] We see an explicit example in the *Şehname-i Âl-i 'Osman* (Book of Kings of the House of Osman), dating from 1590–91.[56] This basic chronology of the Ottoman dynasty, which recounts the reign of each successive sultan, is an incomplete manuscript and has only three finished illustrations. In addition to a long description of the pavilion built by the grand vizier Sinan Paşa for Murad III, the text includes poems praising the grand vizier for his skills as a commander and asking Sinan Paşa for a position.[57] One of the poems Lokman includes in the *Şehname-i Âl-i 'Osman* contrasts the military accomplishments of Sinan Paşa with those of his rival Lala Mustafa Paşa. Lokman is highly critical of Lala Mustafa Paşa and adopts an overly congratulatory attitude toward Sinan Paşa.[58] Lokman's contemporary and critic, Mustafa Âli, on the other hand, adopts the opposite attitude toward the two commanders, praising Lala Mustafa Paşa at the expense of Sinan Paşa.[59] Patronage relation-

---

[54] For a more detailed examination, see Fetvacı, "Viziers to Eunuchs," esp. ch. 3. For the factionalization of the Ottoman court, see Fleischer, *Bureaucrat and Intellectual*.

[55] For other examples, see Fetvacı, "Viziers to Eunuchs."

[56] British Library (hereafter BL), Add. 7931.

[57] BL, Add. 7931, fols. 97a–b, "Devleti efzun ola ömri ziyad/Ta ide Lokmanide mansıbla şad," 177a. See also Charles Rieu, *Catalogue of the Turkish Manuscripts in the British Museum* (London: British Museum, 1888), 186–87.

[58] BL, Add. 7931, fol. 87a.

[59] Fleischer, *Bureaucrat and Intellectual*, 49–51, 89, 135.

ships among authors and courtiers determined much of how Ottoman history was written.

The second volume of the *Şehinşehname*, completed in 1592, includes an ode to the spearhead (*sinan*) in the introductory section. The first illustration accordingly shows Sinan Paşa being appointed as grand vizier and commander.[60] The rest of the manuscript details some battles from the Persian wars and includes many illustrations of the 53-day circumcision feast Sultan Murad arranged in his son's honor.[61] These images emphasize the contributions made by Murad's viziers to the festivities. One by one the paintings feature the fireworks provided by the members of the Imperial Council. This stands in marked contrast to the other visual and verbal documentation of the festivities, the *Surname*, composed by İntizami under the supervision of the chief black eunuch, Mehmed Agha, which clearly presents Murad III as the brilliant center of the Ottoman world order.[62] Comparing these works suggests that in the struggle to determine the Ottoman imperial image, the *şehnameci* was no longer, or at least not exclusively, in the service of the dynasty but rather represented the interests of the bureaucrats in a new court order where the imperial household—with its queen mother, favorite women, princes, and confidantes such as eunuchs and tutors—shared power, and it thus brought in new voices, such as İntizami's, to sing their praises.[63]

Lokman's eulogies to the grand vizier in the second volume of the *Şehinşehname* and the *Şehname-i Âl-i 'Osman* are probably more related to the *şehnameci*'s need to ascertain his position and find a new patron after the demise of Sokollu Mehmed Paşa than to Sinan's active patronage of the author. The 1580s appear to have been a worrisome decade for Lokman. An edict from Murad III telling him to speedily complete the *Hünername* also hints at the sultan's displeasure with his services.[64] It appears that Lokman was searching for a powerful backer, and Sinan Paşa was a very good candidate, especially given his high position and his vast fortune. Lokman's quest does not seem to have ended very well, however, as Talikizade was appointed *şehnameci* along-

---

[60] TSK, B. 200, fol. 19a.

[61] Fols. 9b–10a depict the appointment of Sinan Paşa.

[62] TSK, H. 1344.

[63] For a discussion of the struggle for the determination of the royal image, see Cornell Fleischer, "Between the Lines: Realities of Scribal Life in the Sixteenth Century," in C. Imber and C. Heywood, eds., *Studies in Ottoman History in Honor of Professor V.L. Ménage* (Istanbul: Isis Press, 1994), 45–61. For a detailed comparison of Intizami and Lokman's depictions of the festival, see Fetvacı, "Viziers to Eunuchs," 210–30.

[64] Ahmed Refik, *Onuncu Asr-ı Hicride Istanbul Hayatı* (Istanbul: Enderun Kitabevi, 1988), 35–36.

side him in 1590, and Sinan Paşa appears to have favored Talikizade for the recounting of his Hungarian adventures.

The centrality of patronage relationships at the Ottoman court is nowhere more apparent than in the careers of the *şehnamecis*. Lokman had attained the position with the help of Sokollu Mehmed Paşa and his secretary, Feridun Ahmed. The next *şehnameci*, Talikizade, initially had Osman Paşa's backing, then Sinan Paşa's. And the last person to be appointed to the position had been Sinan Paşa's secretary, Hasan Hükmi.[65] Yet after the deaths of their primary supporters, both Lokman and Talikizade reached out to others in search of patronage. The position of *şehnameci* was not a permanent appointment if the *şehnameci*s themselves were constantly in search of patrons, and non-imperial ones at that!

When we juxtapose the archival documents with the contents of Lokman's work, our current understanding of the *şehnameci* as a "permanent, salaried official" becomes untenable. Instead, the occasional nature of Lokman's work, which we glimpsed at the archives through the ad-hoc gathering of artists under his direction and the use of temporary studios, is clearly related to his eulogies seeking the patronage of viziers and other courtiers. The manuscripts Lokman composed and produced, with their visual and verbal content, addressed a broad circle in the Ottoman court, eulogizing not only the sultan but also others in positions of power.

By the time Lokman had come to office as the third *şehnameci*, because the power-wielders in court were more varied than they had been in 1555, his books had to appeal to a broader group. He had truly become a *court* historian, no longer solely at the service of the dynasty. The slow disintegration of the central organization of the Ottoman court implied that his position was no longer as permanent as had been intended at the outset. In the context of the last quarter of the 16th century, when even the position of the grand vizier had become a revolving door, it is no wonder that Lokman did not feel secure in his predominantly political appointment. Despite the instability of the times, he shaped the Ottoman elite's sense of corporate identity, and he recorded the new hierarchy of the Ottoman court in his role as project director of occasional court histories, harnessing the power of both words and images.

Considering this evidence, one begins to wonder if the word *şehnameci* or *şehnameguy* actually referred to a position or if it functioned more like a label. Was Lokman merely a poet, a member of the *müteferrika*, who happened to write verse histories of the Ottoman court? His income from the gifts given

---

[65] A composite but unfinished illustrated manuscript in the Museum of Turkish and Islamic Art (TIEM 1968) contains a section titled "Münşi'at-ı Hükmi Efendi Katib-i Divan-ı Hazret-i Vezir Sinan Paşa."

when he presented his work was augmented by the assignment of fiefs to him and, after 1589, by the title of *defterdar*. Did that imply that he had no salary as *şehnameci*? Was his supervision of the production of *şehname*s no more than a repetitive version of Mustafa Âli's supervision of the production of the *Nus-retname*? The available evidence does not require us to renounce the existence of the position, but the questions raised above help enrich and expand our current assumptions about the office of *şehnameci*.

Street scene in Istanbul with Süleymaniye Camii in the background, photograph by Sébah and Jouailler, late 19th century (collection of Nezih Başgelen, Istanbul).

2

VOICES OF OPPOSITION IN THE REIGN OF SULTAN SÜLEYMAN
THE CASE OF İBRAHIM PAŞA (1523–36)

EBRU TURAN

Scholars of Ottoman history have maintained that Sultan Süleyman's 46-year reign was the golden age of the Ottoman Empire. According to the prevailing view, the Ottoman Empire attained its cultural, institutional, political, and military zenith under the rule of Sultan Süleyman (r. 1520–66), after which it began an irreversible decline that continued until its final dissolution in 1918. Accompanying this perception of Ottoman history is the sultanic image of Süleyman as the perfect ruler, who brought the Ottoman Empire to its height through his military prowess and political acumen. His regime represented an ideal period of rule portrayed as the perfection of the classical age, during which his subjects and servants lived happily in idyllic order. His impeccable rule was thus beyond political criticism or opposition. There were no significant conflicts or clashes in the political life of the realm, and sultanic power and authority, representative of the state, was neither censured nor challenged.[1] A number of recent studies on the reign of Süleyman have questioned this view of Ottoman history. They have demonstrated that Süleyman's era was not merely the culmination of linear historical development but rather a period of discontinuities and new formations, including the rise of a distinct Ottoman identity and tradition that affected Ottoman art and institutions for centuries to come.[2] Most importantly, these

---

[1] This image of Süleyman and his reign is most often juxtaposed with that of his successors. It has been argued that the sultans following Süleyman were weak and incompetent figures who let the women, courtiers, and eunuchs at the court usurp political power—a development that eventually led to confusion, factionalism, and even violence at the center of Ottoman political life. All of these changes have been considered signs of decline. For example, see Vernon J. Parry, "The Successors of Sulaiman, 1566–1617," in Vernon J. Parry and M. A. Cook, eds. *A History of the Ottoman Empire to 1730: Chapters from the Cambridge History of Islam and the New Cambridge Modern History* (Cambridge: Cambridge University Press, 1976), 103–32; Vernon J. Parry, "The Period of Murād IV, 1617–48," in ibid., 133–56.

[2] Cornell H. Fleischer, *Bureaucrat and Intellectual in the Ottoman Empire: The Historian Mustafa Âli (1541–1600)* (Princeton, NJ: Princeton University Press, 1986); Cornell H. Fleischer, "Between the Lines: Realities of Scribal Life in the Sixteenth Century," in C.

new studies have shown that Süleyman's image as a perfect and ideal ruler was actually an ideological construct rather than a historical reality, developed to consolidate Ottoman claims to universal sovereignty in the 16th century.[3]

Notwithstanding the significance of this revised view, several important questions have yet to be examined. First, how can one transcend the literary image of Süleyman as a quasi-divine figure, the prevailing view found in contemporary Ottoman accounts? Were there voices critical of the sultan and his policies, and if so, how can one recover them? How can one interpret subversive views which appear to have been marginalized by the bourgeoning Ottoman historiography in the reign of Süleyman?

This chapter will suggest an alternative strategy for addressing the above questions. Rather than focus on the sultan himself, I shall examine how negative portrayals of the sultan's powerful grand vizier İbrahim Paşa provide an indirect critique of Süleyman's regime. The most important political figure of Süleyman's reign after the sultan himself, İbrahim Paşa was a man who could be even considered the sultan's alter ego; his acts and policies were seen as representing the will of the sultan. Therefore, critiques of the sultan's most intimate associate, which continued to circulate in public, provide a unique opportunity to uncover dissonance and political opposition during the reign of Süleyman.

İbrahim Paşa is certainly one of the most illustrious and controversial characters of Ottoman history. He was Süleyman's slave and childhood companion from his princely household, and he accompanied his master to the imperial capital when Süleyman ascended the throne in 1520. In 1523, İbrahim was elevated directly from the personal service of the sultan to the grand vizierate, the highest office in the empire, without having served in any military or administrative office beforehand. He occupied this position for 13 years, and throughout the period, he ruled the empire with power equal to that of the sultan. His fall from power, however, was as sudden and unexpected as his rise: he lost not only his position but also his life when Süleyman had him strangled one night in the palace in 1536.[4]

Heywood and C. Imber, eds. *Studies in Ottoman History in Honour of Professor V. L. Ménage* (Istanbul: Isis Press, 1994), 45–61; Cornell H. Fleischer, "The Lawgiver as Messiah: The Making of the Imperial Image in the Reign of Süleyman," in G. Vernstein, ed., *Soliman le Magnifique et son temps* (Paris: La Documentation Français, 1992), 159–77; Gülru Necipoğlu, "A Kanun for the State, a Canon for the Arts: Conceptualizing the Classical Synthesis of Ottoman Art and Architecture," in ibid., 195–216.

[3] Fleischer, "The Lawgiver as Messiah," 171–74.

[4] For İbrahim Paşa, see Hester Donaldson Jenkins, *İbrahim Pasha, Grandvizir of Suleiman the Magnificent* (New York: Columbia University Press, 1911); Tayyib Gökbilgin, "İbrahim Paşa," *İslam Ansiklopedisi*; Feridun Emecen, "İbrahim Paşa," *Diyanet İşleri Vakfı İslam Ansiklopedisi*; Ebru Turan, "The Sultan's Favorite: İbrahim Paşa and the Making of the Ottoman Universal Sovereignty" (Ph.D. dissertation, University of Chicago, 2007).

What sets İbrahim Paşa apart from other Ottoman grand viziers is that he did not have a political career before he was appointed to the empire's highest office. He was designated as grand vizier solely by virtue of his master's affection, favor, and trust for him, rather than his own professional background and past achievements. A creature of the sultan, he owed all that he had—his power, status, rank, and wealth—to Süleyman, and was thus unconditionally dependent on him. Moreover, İbrahim was more than a mere servant or adviser to Süleyman—he was Süleyman's alter ego and inseparable companion. Süleyman presented İbrahim in public not as simply a slave dear to him but his best friend and equal, with whom he wished to share all that he had, including his sultanic authority and prerogatives. İbrahim Paşa's status as the sultan's duplicate found its full articulation in 1529, when Süleyman issued a particular document conferring on İbrahim Paşa the title of *serasker*. Although the term means "commander-in-chief," the royal document reveals that Süleyman created İbrahim Paşa as his full representative who would stand for him in public with full powers as if the sultan himself were present.[5] The destinies of Süleyman and İbrahim were politically, personally, and institutionally intertwined to the extent that it is sometimes not possible to distinguish one from the other. By examining the voices critical of İbrahim Paşa one can begin to identify the contours of political opposition to Süleyman's regime.

This task is extremely challenging, however, because of İbrahim Paşa's special status as the sultan's mirror image. This status led historians of Süleyman's era, whose ultimate aim was to elevate the sultan's imperial image, to extol the virtues of the paşa and to shower him with lavish praises as Süleyman's confidant, chief advisor, and glorious commander. Naturally, the paşa's sudden execution in 1536 on the order of the sultan posed difficulties for contemporary historians, whose task was to justify the sultan's policies. It was impossible to explain İbrahim's fall by criticizing him or to justify it citing his wrong decisions, policies, or deeds, because in the past he had been fully supported and his actions approved by the sultan himself. Sources from this period chose either to ignore the subject or to offer a few vague and unconvincing reasons. For example, it was suggested that İbrahim Paşa's character had suddenly changed, that he had begun to abuse his power, or that he had made some unspecified grave mistakes which in the end greatly vexed the sultan and led him to execute the paşa.[6]

[5] Celālzāde Mustafā, in Petra Kappert, ed. *Geschichte Sultan Süleymān Kānūnīs von 1520 bis 1557, oder Tabakāt ül-Memālik ve Derecāt ül-Mesālik* (Wiesbaden: Steiner, 1981), 179a–82b.

[6] Ibid., 277a–78b; Hüseyin G. Yurdaydın, *Matrakçı Nasuh* (Ankara: Üniversite Basimeri, 1974), 38–39, 57–60; Bostān Çelebi, *Süleymānnāme*, Türk Tarih Kurumu nr. 18, 161a–161b; Senā'ī, *Süleymānnāme*, Topkapı Sarayı Kütüphanesi Revan 1288, 82a–83a.

While conducting research in Istanbul as a John Freely Fellow in 2002–2003, I discovered a number of Ottoman accounts that actually contained remarks highly critical of İbrahim Paşa. The common characteristic of these texts is that they all date from the late 16th or 17th centuries–that is, much later than the period under consideration. Apparently, when all the parties involved were long dead and İbrahim Paşa's case no longer bore immediate political relevance, there was no longer any obstacle to recording alternative accounts that continued to circulate in oral traditions. It is also worth noting that these accounts are either completely anonymous texts or pseudo-continuations of the well-known, politically correct, cleansed narratives. Another group of sources that distinctively include subversive material about İbrahim Paşa are Egyptian histories dating from later periods. İbrahim Paşa's three-month sojourn in Egypt in 1524 appears to have given later historians a convenient vehicle for incorporating information concerning the paşa. It is also striking that the rumors circulating within the circles of Istanbul, which could not be recorded at the imperial center due to political circumstances, were eventually put down on paper in accounts composed at the periphery.

In order to better elucidate the differences between subversive and official accounts sponsored by the imperial court and to explore the broader political and ideological significance of this phenomenon, a few specific examples need to be examined. For that purpose, we shall compare how three important events from the early years of İbrahim Paşa's career were recounted in both types of works–his appointment to the grand vizierate, the revolt of his chief rival Ahmed Paşa in Egypt, and his expedition to Egypt in 1524.

The history of Celalzade Mustafa (d. 1567), the famous chancellor of Sultan Süleyman, is certainly the canonical account for the events of Süleyman's reign. Celalzade was not only a contemporary figure, but thanks to his prominent position in the imperial bureaucracy he was an eyewitness to most of the events he related. These factors give his work great credibility and make him the premier historian cited by later generations. This is especially the case for İbrahim Paşa's grand vizierate, because Celalzade also served the paşa for a short period, as his personal secretary on his trip to Egypt.[7]

According to Celalzade's account, after the dismissal of the Grand Vizier Piri Paşa in 1523, a competent servant of the state had to be found, one capable of undertaking the responsibilities that the grand vizierate demanded. Deeming the present dignitaries of the court unworthy of the office, the sultan instead chose İbrahim, a slave from his princely household, to be his new grand vizier.

[7] For Celalzade, see I. H. Uzunçarşılı, "Onaltıncı Asır Ortalarında Yaşamış Olan İki Büyük Şahsiyet: Tosyalı Celalzade Mustafa ve Salih Çelebiler," *Türk Tarih Kurumu Belleten* 22/87 (1958): 391–441.

İbrahim was not only better qualified for the job, but his loyalty to the sultan was beyond question, considering that he had been groomed and nurtured by Süleyman himself. However, the second vizier Ahmed Paşa, who was known for his conniving and evil disposition, had expected to succeed Piri Paşa. Wracked with jealousy over İbrahim's sudden promotion, Ahmed Paşa demanded as compensation his appointment to be governor-general of Egypt. As soon as he took up his post, the vengeful paşa rebelled against the sultan and proclaimed his independence. His attempt to seize the sultanate of Egypt proved abortive and he was soon caught and executed. After Ahmed Paşa's revolt was put down, İbrahim Paşa was sent to Egypt with the mission of establishing an Ottoman administration that would put the legal, financial, and military affairs of the province in order. Accompanied by other skillful officials, such as the treasurer Iskender Chelebi and the chief secretary of the imperial council, Celalzade Mustafa, İbrahim Paşa fully demonstrated his extraordinary qualities and acumen as a statesman on this mission. He succeeded in bringing law and order to Egypt, a task at which all of his predecessors had failed.[8]

Although modern scholarship has drawn primarily on Celalzade's account, its version of events differs only slightly from other well-known historical works composed in Süleyman's reign.[9] Thus one can safely assume that Celalzade represents a consensus among contemporary historians supporting the official stance of the court. This consensus, however, appears to have been challenged by some less widely known accounts, for instance by *İbtihācü't-tevārīh*, an Ottoman historical work from the late 16th century.[10]

It has been suggested that the *İbtihāc* is a continuation of another late 16th century work, *Tacü't-tevārīh*, a history composed by Hoca Sadeddin, the tutor of Murad III.[11] Internal evidence suggests that the work's alternative account of the Ottoman history for the period of 1520–26 has little relation to the work of Hoca Sadeddin and is in fact very different from the standard accounts. What sets the work apart from the others is *İbtihāc's* extremely critical stance on İbrahim Paşa. The text ends abruptly in the middle of a sentence while describing the battle of Mohacs in 1526; this is followed by a blank page, which appears to mark the tran-

---

[8] Celālzāde, 109b–15b, 121a–30a; Snjezana Buzov, "The Lawgiver and his Lawmakers: The Role of Legal Discourse in the Change of Ottoman Imperial Culture" (Ph.D. dissertation, University of Chicago, 2005), 29–42, 214–18.

[9] Hadîdî, *Tevârih-i Âl-i Osman (1299-1523)*, ed. Necdet Öztürk (Istanbul: Edebiyat Fakültesi Basımevi, 1991), 443–56; Bostân, 54a–66a; Seyyid Muhammed es-Seyyid Mahmud, *XVI. Asırda Mısır Eyaleti* (Istanbul: Edebiyat Fakültesi Basımevi, 1990), 77–81.

[10] *İbtihācü't-tevārīh*, Süleymaniye Hüsrev Paşa, 321 and 322.

[11] M. Münir Aktepe, "İbtihâcü't-Tevârih," *İstanbul Üniversitesi Tarih Dergisi* 10, 14 (1959): 71–84.

sition to a much later period, beginning at 1551.[12] Thus the most important years of İbrahim Paşa's grand vizierate (1526–36) are missing! The unfinished sentence and the blank page hint that the *İbtihāc* incorporated additional parts relating the events of these years, but due to their subversive content, they were later removed.

It would seem that the *İbtihāc* was originally an anonymous account whose writer concealed his identity in order to freely communicate his critical political views. Through forging a pseudo-link with the canonical account of the *Tācü't-tevārīh*, the author of the *İbtihāc* passed off his text as an unsubversive account of Ottoman history, and thus it remained in circulation. The existence of a few extant copies in Turkish and European libraries proves that the survival strategies that the text employed in fact turned out to be effective.

A number of specific examples demonstrate how the *İbtihāc*'s account of İbrahim Paşa's early years in the grand vizierate diverges from the orthodox narratives. First, unlike Celalzade, who claims that İbrahim Paşa was designated as grand vizier because he had some extraordinary qualities that no other royal servant possessed, the *İbtihāc* maintains that it was in fact İbrahim Paşa's guile and deceit which brought him to power. In order to reach the grand vizierate, İbrahim first approached the second vizier Ahmed Paşa and gained his friendship. Ahmed Paşa, supported by İbrahim, then convinced the sultan to dismiss the third vizier Ferhad Paşa, another eligible candidate for the grand vizierate. Afterward, İbrahim and Ahmed Paşa began to conspire against the Grand Vizier Piri Paşa, and finally persuaded Süleyman to send Piri Paşa into retirement. İbrahim, however, turned against Ahmed Paşa at this moment and convinced Süleyman to appoint him rather than Ahmed to the grand vizierate.[13]

Similarly, the *İbtihāc* also gives an entirely different account of Ahmed Paşa's revolt in Egypt, one that aims to exonerate Ahmed Paşa. Ahmed Paşa is portrayed as a brave man who fell victim to political intrigue and İbrahim Paşa's enmity. Conspiring to have Ahmed Paşa killed, İbrahim Paşa entrusted one of his aides with the execution of Ahmed Paşa and sent him to Egypt with a secret order. Through his connections in Istanbul, Ahmed Paşa got wind of the plot against his life, and he rebelled out of desperation in order to save his life. Hence, it was not Ahmed Paşa's disloyalty that turned him into a traitor, as Celalzade claims, but rather İbrahim Paşa's threatening intrigues.[14]

The part of the *İbtihāc* concerning İbrahim Paşa's expedition to Egypt also contradicts Celalzade's story. Celalzade singles out İbrahim Paşa as the architect of the great success in ordering the affairs of Egypt. In contrast, the *İbtihāc* states that in the first year of his appointment, İbrahim Paşa was in agony because he

---

[12] *İbtihāc*, Hüsrev Paşa 322, 77a–78a. The folio 77b is blank, and 78a moves directly to the year 958/1551. Aktepe notes that this is the case in all the extant copies.

[13] Ibid., 321, 121b–22b.   [14] Ibid., 123a–32b.

lacked the competence that his office demanded. Even worse, most of the time he could not conceal his incapacity. Therefore, in order to cover his defects and at the same time to obtain practical experience in government affairs, he requested to be sent to Egypt.[15]

Other Ottoman accounts challenge Celalzade's depiction of İbrahim Paşa as the sole hero of the whole mission. For instance, Diyarbekri, an eyewitness of İbrahim Paşa's visit to Egypt, made the following remark in regard to İbrahim Paşa's dealings in Cairo: "The late İbrahim Paşa existed only in name. It was İskender Çelebi, the treasurer at the sultan's threshold, who managed all the affairs.... People would refer to him for every matter, and without him no business could be completed."[16]

Although the differences between the earlier and later accounts of İbrahim Paşa in Egypt are striking, they invite additional questions. How can one interpret the critical views on İbrahim Paşa found in the later sources? Do they merely represent the opinions of the paşa's personal enemies; or do they illustrate the political sensitivities of a broader milieu within the society? Most importantly, what are the implications of these negative remarks about İbrahim Paşa for Süleyman and his sultanic authority?

In order to examine these questions at greater length we turn to the invaluable information on Ottoman politics at Istanbul found in Venetian sources of the early 16th century. By the 16th century, the Venetians had established themselves as the chief Mediterranean power controlling the east-west long-distance trade passing through Ottoman lands, the central point of which was Istanbul. A considerable Venetian community resided in the city, governed by a Venetian official known as the *bailo*. The *bailo* also functioned as a permanent political representative at the Ottoman court and passed news from Istanbul to Venice on a regular basis.[17] In addition, through the community's connections within the larger urban setting of Istanbul, the *bailo* had direct access to the political debates that dominated public life in the imperial capital.

Venetian accounts from the early 16th century are rich in information on Ottoman political life, and they provide unique reports regarding İbrahim Paşa. The election of Charles of Habsburg as the new Holy Roman Emperor in 1519

[15] Ibid., 139b.

[16] Diyārbekrī Abdüssamed b. Seyyidī Ali b. Dāvud, *Nevādirü't-tevārih*, Millet Ali Emiri Tarih, no. 596, 436b. Diyārbekrī's history spans a period from the the first Muslim conquest of Egypt through 945/1538–39. The author himself is a 16th century character; he knew İskender Çelebi personally. For a brief description of this work, see Seyyid Muhammed, *XVI. Asırda Mısır Eyaleti* (Istanbul: Marmara Üniversitesi Fen-Edebiyat Fakültesi, 1990): 18–19.

[17] Eric Dursteler, *Venetians in Constantinople: Nation, Identity, and Coexistence in the Early Modern Mediterranean* (Baltimore, MD: Johns Hopkins University Press, 2006), 23–40.

put the Republic into a precarious position, as Venice suddenly found herself surrounded by Habsburg-controlled territories. In order to stand up to the Habsburgs in Italy, the Venetians sought Ottoman support, prompting an increase in diplomatic activity on the part of Venice, which included the frequent dispatches of extraordinary envoys (*orators*) to the Ottoman court, a closer observation of the Ottoman politics at the center, and the establishment of friendly relations with key Ottoman officials in order to gain their favor. İbrahim Paşa was a great ally of the Republic in Istanbul, and during his grand vizierate the Ottomans pursued an exceptionally pro-Venetian foreign policy. For that reason, the Venetians had a particular interest in İbrahim Paşa and closely followed his affairs.[18]

Their interest was not related solely to political concerns. İbrahim himself was originally a Venetian subject from Parga, a small town on the western coast of Greece. He had been captured as a young boy in the late 15th century in an Ottoman raid, enslaved, converted to Islam, and presented to Süleyman as a gift. The Venetians were both fascinated and intrigued to see their once-humble subject, the son of a simple sailor, climb to the highest office in the Ottoman Empire. Therefore, their accounts reveal many details about İbrahim, his origins, his intimacy with Süleyman, the reception of his power and authority in public, all of which are either completely missing or deliberately omitted from the Ottoman sources.[19]

The Venetian sources reveal that İbrahim Paşa's sudden elevation to the grand vizierate aroused an intense public debate in Istanbul, centering on the sultan's decision to appoint İbrahim directly from his personal service in the privy chamber to the highest office in the empire. Apparently, İbrahim Paşa's swift rise was widely resented and publicly criticized. For instance, Pietro Zen, the Venetian ambassador who arrived in Istanbul in June 1523, noted that after İbrahim's designation as grand vizier, people in Istanbul began to complain about the Ottoman government. He heard people saying, "No attempts are being made to find the criminals who have committed crimes, such as rape, murder, or robbery. The government no longer has the reputation as it had before." Zen then adds, "The Turks themselves are saying that a great ruin will befall the House of Osman because one can say that the empire is mostly governed by good fortune rather than by Süleyman and İbrahim's prudence. None of the old slaves is left in the court, but all have been sent out to the provinces. They first say that Piri Paşa should return to his prime position … due to his being well versed in the affairs of the empire, astute in government, experienced in the conditions of the world, and wise and prudent."[20]

[18] Turan, "Sultan's Favorite," 269–80.   [19] Ibid., 122–42.

[20] R. Fulin, "Itinerario di ser Piero Zen stato orator al serenissimo Signor turcho fatto per io Marin Sanuto in sumario," *Archivio Veneto* 22 (1881): 117.

In a similar manner to the above-cited *İbtihāc*, the Venetian sources state that the inhabitants of the city blamed İbrahim for the dismissal or execution of the chief paşas who had held the highest offices in the empire before İbrahim Paşa's appointment. Süleyman dismissed his most experienced and capable grand vizier, Piri Paşa upon İbrahim's wishes. The third vizier, Ferhad Paşa, who was also the sultan's son-in-law, likewise had the misfortune of being an enemy of İbrahim Paşa, and he was soon demoted and subsequently executed.[21] Most interestingly, the Venetian accounts show that Ahmed Paşa's revolt created a controversy in Istanbul. There were even those who rejoiced at the news of Ahmed Paşa's revolt and held İbrahim Paşa responsible for it. A Venetian report from Istanbul noted, "The old slaves were pleased to hear of Ahmed Paşa's revolt as it seemed to them that it would lead to İbrahim Paşa's shame since he sent Ahmed Paşa to Cairo. Moreover, being a warlike man and experienced in government, Ahmed Paşa, people thought, would not have taken such an action if he had not had a strong foundation for it."[22]

The striking similarities between the contemporary Venetian accounts, the compilers of which were first-hand observers of the events, and the Ottoman texts written in a much later period indicate that the later Ottoman accounts should not be dismissed as inaccurate or distorted late sources. Nor do they appear to represent only the views of a few personal enemies of the paşa. In fact, the Venetian sources support the argument that the late indigenous sources accurately mirror political discussions and controversies of an earlier period suppressed by official Ottoman accounts.

The standard accounts from the reign of Süleyman suppressed these debates because ultimately it was the reputation of Sultan Süleyman that had to be protected. It was the sultan's decision to raise İbrahim to the grand vizierate. Likewise it was the sultan who dismissed all the other paşas from their offices, sent Ahmed to Egypt, and executed Ferhad. However, a closer analysis of the criticisms directed at İbrahim Paşa would reveal that there was more at stake than just the appointment of a slave to the grand vizierate. The debate triggered by the rise of İbrahim Paşa had important ideological implications and directly concerned the nature of sultanic authority.

İbrahim's sudden elevation to the grand vizierate was not welcomed by his contemporaries because by the early 16th century the Ottoman military and

---

[21] Ibid., 110; Marino Sanudo, *I diarii di Marino Sanuto (MCCCCXCVI-MDXXXIII) dall' autografo Marciano ital. cl. VII codd. CDXIX-CDLXXVII*, pubblicati per cura di Rinaldo Fulin, Federico Stefani, Nicolò Barozzi, Guglielmo Berchet, Marco Allegri; 58 vols., 37 (Venezia: R. Deputazione veneta di storia patria, 1879–1903), cols. 481, 485; 41, cols 530–31 (hereafter Sanudo).

[22] Sanudo, 36, col. 100.

administrative organization had become highly professionalized. Experience and know-how, in addition to the sultan's favor, had become requirements for holding a high-ranking office in the government, and this fact shaped the elite's expectations for professional advancement. Piri, Ferhad, and Ahmed Paşa were all men of prominence, not only because they held vizieral rank but also because they had made names for themselves through their own achievements. In the early 16th century, the person of an office holder was still more important than the office itself.[23]

İbrahim could not be compared with these paşas. He had assumed no administrative or military office prior to his elevation to the grand vizierate. He was made grand vizier not because of his competence in state affairs but solely because of his master's favor. As the sultan's favorite, İbrahim's swift rise to power represented both an unusual situation in Ottoman politics and a total disregard for the elite's ideals and expectations. It is not difficult to understand why many resented Süleyman's decision.

Articulated in a different way, this resentment cost Süleyman his most capable men in government, created a general distrust for his reign, and led to unnecessary expenditures of vast military and financial resources; the sultan even came close to losing the whole of Egypt. One wonders why Süleyman ventured to promote his favorite to the grand vizierate to begin with. Was his decision primarily a result of his endless love and trust for İbrahim, or did he simply underestimate the consequences of his action? What other incentives could have induced Süleyman to undertake such a risky action?

İbrahim Paşa's unprecedented rise to the grand vizierate was closely related to the creation of unprecedented authority for the sultan, which could be indifferent to socially and politically sanctioned norms. The sultan could disregard merit and competence as conditions of social mobility and constitute rank and status through his own favor. In this way, the sultan's will and personal power came to supersede everything else, and he came to be defined as the sole force in the formation of public order.[24]

This new, unprecedented image of the sultan with absolute power was sanctioned in the 1520s when Süleyman had just ascended the throne. Following Sultan Selim's defeat of Shah Ismail of Persia in 1514 and his stunning conquests of Syria and Egypt in 1516 and 1517, as well as the election of Charles of Habsburg as the Holy Roman Emperor in 1519, the Ottoman dynasty began to assert more aggressively than before that world rule belonged to the Ottoman sultan

---

[23] Turan, "Sultan's Favorite," 184–88.

[24] Ibid., 203–10. On the similar debates in early modern European context, see Curtis Perry, "The Politics of Access and Representation of the Sodomite King in Early Modern England," *Renaissance Quarterly* 53, 4 (Winter 2000): 1054–83.

because God had ordained him to establish a universal empire uniting mankind under a single rule and faith.[25]

One important constituent of this new Ottoman imperial ideology was the refashioning of the sultan as the manifestation of God's will on earth, a quality that further endowed him with a god-like image. As closeness to God granted power, distinction, and authority, those who enjoyed the sultan's favor, protection, and intimacy were similarly celebrated as the most distinguished. Thus İbrahim's unprecedented rise to the grand vizierate was closely intertwined with the creation of a divine image for Süleyman. It is not surprising that those who believed in the divine mandate of Süleyman were the same who gave full support to İbrahim Paşa's grand vizierate. By the same token, the most committed champions of the Ottoman imperialism in the early 16th century also assumed the task of responding to those who questioned Süleyman's right to bring his favorite to the highest office in the empire.

The most famous of them was probably Celalzade himself. Both in his history as well as in the preamble to the *Kānūnnāme* (code of laws) of Egypt which he penned in 1525 during İbrahim Paşa's mission in Egypt, Celalzade tried to justify İbrahim's appointment by developing an explicit parallel between God and the sultan's power to grant distinction by favoring some over others. Just as İbrahim's Quranic namesake Abraham was chosen by God, given the rank of prophet–a demonstration of his closeness to God and thereby his distinction above others, as reflected in his epithet of *Halīl Allāh* (friend of God)–İbrahim likewise became the sultan's intimate companion with whom the sultan shared all his personal affairs, including those pertinent to the administration of the empire. Yet, by attributing superhuman qualifications to İbrahim, Celalzade also wanted to assure that proximity to the sultan indicated one's superb virtues and abilities, for the sultan granted his favor only to those who really deserved it.[26]

Another Ottoman author who sought to legitimize İbrahim Paşa's rise to power via sultanic favor was a certain Sa'di bin 'Abdü'l-Müteal.[27] In his history spanning the years from 1511 through 1525, Sa'di claimed that the sultan's will was a manifestation of God's will and thus those who enjoyed the sultan's benev-

---

[25] Fleischer, "Ottoman and Habsburg Empires in the Sixteenth Century: Is Translation Needed?" Conference paper, Imperial Models in the Early Modern World, Part 2: Managing Difference in Early Modern Empires (UCLA, February 9-10, 2007); Turan, "Sultan's Favorite," 145–79, 265–69.

[26] Buzov, "Lawgiver," 214–18.

[27] The identity of the author is unknown. It is possible that he could be the Şeyhülislam Sa'dī Çelebi, who lived in the first half of the 16th century and was also a protégé of İbrahim Paşa. On Sa'dī Çelebi, see Richard Cooper Repp, *The Müfti of Istanbul: A Study in the Development of the Ottoman Learned Hierarchy* (London: Ithaca Press for the Board of the Faculty of Oriental Studies, Oxford University, 1986), 240–44.

olence were also blessed by God.[28] Hence, these official accounts which modern historians have heretofore regarded as the sole representatives of Ottoman historiography in the reign of Süleyman were to some degree a reaction and response to contemporary political debates carried on in the capital city, questioning the decisions and deeds of the sultan.[29]

It seems that by the early 16th century there was already a substantial awareness of and involvement in politics among the city populace of Istanbul. Ottoman subjects in the city were both interested in and informed about the political life of the Ottoman court and its dependents. Residents of Istanbul were eager to express their opinions and developed strategies to record and disseminate their ideas; otherwise, as we have seen in the case of the *İbtihāc*, their views might not have come down to us. Most importantly, their critical views did not necessarily imply an animosity toward the Ottoman sultan. On the contrary, their criticism was based on direct concern for the well-being and future existence of royal authority.

The various social, cultural, and political changes in the Ottoman Empire occurring in the first half of the 16th century, such as an enormous increase in literary production and history writing, burgeoning growth of the court's patronage for arts and artists, and an unprecedented display of imperial pomp and majesty did not represent isolated phenomena but rather appear as a response to increasing public opinion in the imperial capital.[30]

Like their counterparts in early modern Europe, the Ottoman rulers of the period tried to control and manipulate the political ideas of their subjects. They also amply employed the medium of art, both in its visual and literary forms, to impose their own ideology on the public.[31] The image prevailing today of Süleyman as world-ruler, divorced from all human weakness and blemish, thus appears in the histories of his period as a construct—one that emerged at least in

---

[28] Sa'dī b. 'Abdü'l-Müte'āl, *Selīmnāme*, TKS Revan 1277, 162a.

[29] For an overview of Ottoman history writing in the reign of Süleyman, see Abdülkadir Özcan, "Historiography in the Reign of Süleyman the Magnificent," in Tülay Duran, ed., *The Ottoman Empire in the Reign of Süleyman the Magnificent* (Istanbul: Historical Research Foundation Istanbul Research Center, 1988), 167–222 ; Robert Mantran, "L'historiographie ottoman a l'epoque de Soliman le Magnifique," in Veinstein, ed., *Soliman le Magnifique et son temps*, 25–32.

[30] For a summary of the historiographical debates on the development of the public sphere in the European context see Dena Goodman, "Public Sphere and Private Life: Toward a Synthesis of Current Historiographical Approaches to the Old Regime," *History and Theory* 31, 1 (1992): 1–20.

[31] For the similar developments in the Venetian context, see Edward Muir, "Images of Power: Art and Pageantry in Renaissance Venice," *American Historical Review* 84 (1979): 16–52.

part as a response to the concerns of the wider urban setting of Istanbul in the 16th century. Perhaps this assessment could prompt a reconsideration of the Ottoman sultanate as oriental despotism, represented only by the sultan and his conquering power, and recognition of the silent agents behind the rise of the Ottoman state and the process of empire building, whose voices have largely remained unheard.*

*I would like to thank Dr. Sara Yildiz from Bilgi University for her invaluable comments and editorial help.

Street scene in Istanbul, from a late 19th century postcard (collection of Nezih Başgelen, Istanbul).

3

THE HISTORY OF NAMING THE OTTOMAN/TURKISH SABBATIANS

CENGIZ SISMAN

The aim of this chapter is to trace the origin of the term, *Dönme*, often translated as convert or turncoat, the most famous appellation used for naming and describing the Ottoman and Turkish Sabbatian communities. Although much has been written on the Sabbatian movement, only a few scholars have addressed the formation and development of the Sabbatian sect. Hoping to fill this scholarly gap, my dissertation, "A Jewish Messiah in the Ottoman Court: Sabbatai Sevi and Emergence of the Messianic Judeo-Islamic Community in the Seventeenth-Century Ottoman Empire," examined new sources and developed new methodological approaches to different periods of the Sabbatian movement and its subsequent sectarian life.[1] However, there are still a number of unresolved issues with regard to the later history of the Sabbatians. For example, did the Ottoman Sabbatians really vanish from sight in the 18th and 19th centuries, as is often assumed? What was their relation to the surrounding Jewish and Islamic communities? Did they modify their principles as they interacted with the other communities, or remain the same? How did they transmit their enigmatic identity to the next generations? When and why were they called by different names, including *Dönme*s, *Avdeti*s, and *Selanikliler*? When were the names of the sub-sects canonized?

Here I shall deal primarily with the last two questions and argue that Sabbatian communities were called "dönmes" from the beginning, since it was a common practice to identify new converts as such. As the outside world learned more about the distinct character of the Sabbatian version of Islam, the suspicion around the community grew, and the Muslim Turks continued to use the term as a proper noun, *Dönme*, with a connotation of crypto belief and practices, beginning already in the 18th century. In addition to the term *Dönme*, a plethora of other names were used to denote the community by outsiders and the Sabbatians themselves. This is also the case for the names of the sub-sects,

[1] Cengiz Sisman, "A Jewish Messiah in the Ottoman Court: Sabbatai Sevi and Emergence of a Messianic Judeo-Islamic Community in the Seventeenth-Century Ottoman Empire" (Ph.D. dissertation, Harvard University, 2005).

and the terms *Yakubiler, Karakaşlar,* and *Kapancılar* became standard appella-
tions only in the 20th century.

THE FORMATION OF SABBATIAN SECTARIAN LIFE

Before delving into the history of the term(s), I would like to give a brief description of the formation of the Sabbatian sects. The rise of the Sabbatian Jewish
messianic movement in 1665-66 in the Ottoman Empire is one of the most
striking events in early modern history. The Sabbatian movement began when
Sabbatai Sevi, a man educated in Jewish mysticism, proclaimed himself the Messiah in Turkey in May 1665. At a time when religion mattered above all, many
were intoxicated by the messianic fervor, halted the course of their daily lives,
sold all their valuables and took to the roads, aiming to join the first ranks
behind the Messiah on the way to the Promised Land, Jerusalem. Soon, however,
the great expectation was irrevocably shattered, due to the unexpected and sudden conversion of the Messiah to Islam in 1666. Sabbatai Sevi became Aziz
Mehmed Efendi in new Ottoman garments.

Even though the movement came to an end when the "messiah" was forced to
convert to Islam by the Ottoman authorities, it had an enduring impact on the
collective memory of larger Jewish communities all over the world. After the
conversion, the complexity of Sabbatianism manifested itself in Judaism, Islam
and Christianity, as Elisheva Carlebach would call it, "heretical theology" and
"sectarianism."

After the death of "the converted Messiah" in 1676, some of his believers
developed a sectarian life and apocalyptic theology mixed with Jewish, Christian
and Islamic beliefs and rituals. Between 1676 and 1720, the community of
believers split into three sub-sects because of disputes over the matters of
authenticity and authority.[2] Meanwhile the main center of Sabbatian activities
moved to Salonika, where it remained until 1924.

It is true that the early Sabbatians converted to Islam not necessarily because
of the conviction but because of their imminent messianic expectations. When
the allegedly imminent salvation did not happen, they, like many other messianic communities, started to conform to the principles of surrounding communities. Even in the formative period, although the community took its
principal doctrines from the Jewish mystical tradition, it adopted its structural
format from the Islamic Sufi tradition. After centuries of interaction with the
larger society, community members became not only *dervish*es in but also *sheyhs*
among the *Mevlevi, Bektaşi,* and *Melami* Sufi orders. During this long process,
the Ottoman Jewish-Sabbatian culture was slowly transformed into an Ottoman

---

[2] I am able to unearth a possible fourth Sabbatian sub-sect, which I tentatively call *Berga-
malılar*; see Sisman, "Jewish Messiah."

Islamic-Sabbatian culture. As Bernard Septimus emphasizes in his analysis of the transition of Hispano-Jewish culture from Islam to Christianity in Spain during the 13th century, "continuity and change are not contradictory historical categories: in a changing context the old can play new roles and the new assumes the old."[3] The formative period of the Ottoman Sabbatian communities and their subsequent developments showed great resemblances to the crypto-Jewish Marrano communities, who were "forced" Jewish converts in Spain and Portuguese in the 15th and 16th centuries. Some scholars go so far as to call the Ottoman Sabbatians "voluntary Marranos," since they converted to Islam not by coercion but by choice.[4]

A recently found manuscript at Harvard University, for example, shows a level of interaction between the Sabbatians and the Sufis, already in the middle of the 18th century. According to this manuscript, it seems that both kabbalistic and Sufi hymns were sung together in their rituals. A rabbinic *responsa* from 1765, which reads "is it permissible to write amulets for apostates among us who have long been infringing the commands of God and still persist in their heresy, desecrate the Sabbath, and eat impure food, and have the power to escape these persecutions, as so many of them have done and continue to adhere to the laws of Moses?" also illustrates both the Sabbatian relation to their old communities, as well as their conformity in their new community.

The community was not a secret community as was assumed in the 18th and 19th centuries. Sabbatian communities were known as *Dönmes* from the beginning. And almost every consul in the town, or every traveler who passed through town, did not fail to recognize the existence of a "half-Turkish, half-Jewish" community. We have many accounts of missionaries such as Souciet,[5] Brewer[6] and Schaufler;[7] travelers such as Niebuhr,[8] Leake,[9] McFarlane,[10]

[3] B. Septimus, *Hispano-Jewish Culture in Transition* (Cambridge, MA: Harvard University Press, 1982).

[4] Despite the similarities between the Marrano and Sabbatian experience, there are several important differences between the two communities on the level of intentions, means, and aims.

[5] P. Jean-Baptiste Souciet, "De la ville Salonique, par le P. Jean-Babtiste Souciet, de la compaigne de Jesus, missionnaire au Levant [in 1734]," in *Jesuits*, ed. Aime-Martin (Paris, 1838).

[6] J. Brewer, *A Residence at Constantinople in the Year 1827* (New Haven, 1830).

[7] William Schauffler 1798-1883, "Shabbathai Zevi and His Followers," *Journal of American Oriental Society* 2 (1851); 3-26. (I am preparing this article for republication with an introduction).

[8] Carsten Niebuhr, "Von Vershidenen Nationen und Religionparthien im Turkichen Reiche," *Deutsches Museum, Siebendes Stuct* (July 1784), 1-23.

[9] W. Leake, *Travels in Northern Greece*, 4 vols. (London, 1835).

[10] C. MacFarlane, *Constantinople in 1828* (London, 1829).

Ubicini,[11] Hartmann,[12] and ambassadors such as Arasy[13] and Cousinéry,[14] from the 18th and 19th centuries, who were able to talk to members of the community and gather information about the communal life and principles of the Ottoman Sabbatians. These are not always detailed accounts, but together they allow us to safely argue that the community did not disappear from sight. It was instead an "open secret" for outsiders.[15]

By the 19th century, more and more references appeared in the Ottoman official archival sources. A document from the Ottoman archive, dated 16 Zilhicce 1278 (14 June 1862), for example, suggests that, on the official level, the Ottoman authorities acknowledged the existence of such a group, but did not take any position against these idiosyncratic Muslims. Another document, dated 1309 (1891), confirms this observation. Ahmet Rifat, in his *Lugat-i Tarihiyye ve Coğrafiyye*,[16] describes the community without passing any judgment. On the popular level, however, there was a growing negative perception of the Ottoman Sabbatians, as seen in the 1873 treatise of Ahmed Safi, who argued that Sabbatian dissimulation was a grave threat to the Ottoman Muslim community.

There are also many tractates and newspaper entries which were written by both Sabbatians and anti-Sabbatians at the beginning of the 20th century, when the community still had its traditional structure. These sources also make various references to the Sabbatian communities.

A HISTORY OF NAMING THE SABBATIANS

Naming Ottoman Sabbatian communities had always been an intriguing question since its inception. Many epithets coined to identify them frequently suggested both the circumstances of their conversion and their degree of adherence to Judaism. The communities called themselves *Ma'aminim* (believers), *Haverim* (friends), *Ba'ale-i Milhama* (Warriors), or each sub-sect called itself with specific names. The Jews called them *Minim* (heretics), *Mamzerim* (illegal progeny), and *Ma'aminiko*, without making any difference among the subgroups. This much is clear, but what did the Ottomans call them? When did the derogatory term *Dönme* (Turncoats) with the upper case "D" designate the Sabbatian believers?

[11] A. Ubicini, 1818-1884, *Letters on Turkey* (New York, 1973).

[12] M. Hartmann, *Der Islamiche Orient.* 3 vols.; III: *Unpolitische Briefe aus der Turkei* (Leipzig, 1909-1910).

[13] J.V. Arasy (1777), "Description des pays du department du consulat de Salonique," in *Salonique à la fin du XVIIIe siècle*, ed. Michael Laskaris (Athens, 1939).

[14] E. Cousinéry, *Voyage dans la Macédoine* (Paris, 1831).

[15] I am preparing an article on "Sabbatian Life in Salonica as Reflected in Travel Literature and Missionary Accounts."

[16] Ahmet Rifat, *Lugat-i Tarihiyye ve Coğrafiyye*, 4 vols. (Istanbul, 1299), 20.

And when did the outsiders become aware of the differences among the sub-sects? The question of what they were called is quite important because the nomenclature may reveal how they were perceived from the outside.

Immediately after the Sabbatian conversion in the last quarter of the 17th century, the Ottomans must have called them *Nev-Muslim* (New Muslim) or *mühtedi* (the one who attained the truth [by the grace of God]), since all the new converts were identified by those terms in the official records. On a popular level, however, the term *dönme* with a lower case "d" might have been used to designate them, since it was also a common practice.

How the new converts were perceived by the Muslims in general is not easy to determine. We do not know whether they were under the constant scrutiny of the Ottoman religious authorities or "old Muslims" or whether there was any suspicion about the authenticity of their conversions. About the well-being of the new converts, there were mixed reports. Some Christian travelers/observers such as Paul Rycaut and Elias Habesci[17] tend to argue that the converts were treated as second class citizens, and that they were belittled by the larger Muslim community. Conversion had been an everyday phenomenon in the Ottoman Empire, and new converts could find a place in every compartment of state and society according to their merits. More importantly, the terms *mühtedi, Nev-Muslim* or *dönme* were supposed to be dropped in designating the offspring of the converts, since it was assumed that conversion had been completed in the second generation. Hayatizade Mustafa, the physician-in-chief at the palace, who was a Jewish convert himself in the 17th century, constitutes an interesting example. His sons and grandsons, following the family tradition, became physicians-in-chief, and even the *Şeyhülislam*, the greatest religious authority in the Ottoman Islam.[18] This and similar examples could show that the second generation of converts could become fully "naturalized" in Ottoman society.

The Sabbatian believers, after conversion to Islam, were careful in complying with Islamic rules and regulations. It is also highly likely that most of them went through the same evolving conversion experience that Sabbatai Mehmed had gone through. Hence it is hard to assume that the Ottomans doubted the authenticity of their conversion and called them *Dönme*, with a crypto connotation at the very beginning. The term *Dönme*, with a capital "D" which could mean a crypto-Sabbatian must have been coined at a later period, when outsiders, including both Jews and Muslims, started to see the members of the com-

---

[17] Paul Rycaut, *The History of the Turkish Empire* (London, 1687); Elias Habesci, *The Present State of the Ottoman Empire* (London: R. Baldwin, 1784).

[18] For Hayatizade Mustafa Efendi and his progeny, see Cengiz Sisman "A Sephardic Prodigy: Moshe ben Avravanel or Hayatizade Mustafa Efendi, the Physician-in-Chief of the Palace," in Proceedings of *Birinci Ispanyol-Türk-Seferadi Tarih ve Kültür Bulusması*, 2007.

munity acting somewhat differently than the other converts. Hence the outside community did not drop the term *dönme*, instead they used the term *Dönme* for the succeeding generations.

The term *Dönme*, with an uppercase "D," in various spellings was already seen in the writings of missionaries and travelers who visited Salonica at the end of the 18th century. Although it was possible that Salonican people called the community *Dönme*, starting from the 18th century, we do not see the term in available Ottoman records until the second half of the 19th century. The specific meaning of the term *Dönme* would have probably sounded very outlandish for the Ottomans who had not live in Salonica. By the 19th century, the Sabbatian phenomenon became visible and noticed beyond Salonica, but more than *Dönme*, the Ottoman general public preferred to use the term *Avdeti* to refer to them. In the 20th century, however, the Ottoman Sabbatian believers were unanimously called *Dönmes* by outsiders, with a clear connotation of crypto-Sabbatianism and Judaism. With the two treatises published in 1919 titled "Dönmeler" and "Dönmeliğin Hakikati,"[19] the term *Dönme* became part of everyday language. The term was thoroughly imprinted on the Turkish mind, when the *Karakaş* Affair triggered a long chain of discussion about the *Dönmes* in 1924.[20]

The earliest available record to indicate that already in the 18th century the Ottomans referred to the group as the "Dolmäh" belongs to Carsten Niebuhr, a Dutch traveler, who visited Salonica in the 1770s.[21] Because of the paucity of Ottoman sources on the Sabbatian communities from the 18th century, however, it is better to look at the Ottoman dictionaries for the terms *Dönme* and

---

[19] Anonymous, *Dönmeler* (İstanbul: Şems Matbaası, 1919); Binbaşı Sadık, *Dönmeliğin Hakikati* (Dersaadet: Garabet Matbaası, 1919). These texts are rendered into Latin alphabets several times. See for example, E. Düzdağ, *Yakın Tarihimizde Dönmelik ve Dönmeler* (Istanbul, 2003); Ahmet Almaz, *Tarihin Esrarengiz Bir Sayfası* (Istanbul, 2002).

[20] After World War I, Turkey and Greece engaged in a long-standing dispute about their minority populations. The issue was resolved when both sides agreed to exchange Turko-Muslims from Greece with Orthodox Christians from Turkey. According to a rough estimate, 400,000 Turko-Muslims and 1,500,000 Orthodox Christians were uprooted and relocated in Greece and Turkey. Because the *Dönmes* were passed as Turks, they were moved to Turkey. Karakaşzade Mehmed Efendi, who was of Sabbatian origin, lodged a petition to the Turkish parliament, calling on his people to give up their secret life style, and embrace the new, modern Turkish culture. His petition triggered a long discussion, the results of which were published in Turkish newspapers, such as *Vatan*, *Sebilürreşad*, *Resimli Dünya*, and *Son Saat*. The full text of the petition was published in the newspaper *Vakit* in January 1924.

[21] C. Niebuhr, "Von Vershidenen Nationen und Religionparthien im Turkichen Reiche." Carsten Niebuhr (1733-1815) is one of the pioneers of Oriental studies. His works have long been regarded as classics on the geography, the people, the antiquities, and the archaeology of the district of Arabia that he traversed.

Avdeti, and to try to understand what that term would have meant in the 17th, 18th and 19th centuries. Additionally, examining the descriptions of foreign observers is another avenue to trace the historical adventure of the terms *Dönme* and *Avdeti*.

The term *Dönme* (دونمه), is not found in every Ottoman dictionary of the 16th and 17th centuries. For example, the famous 16th century dictionary, *Ahter-i Kebīr* does not have an entry for *Dönme* or *Avdeti*. The first dictionary I was able to locate the term is that of Meninski, which is an indispensable source for the 17th century. It gives a very detailed description of the term *dönme*:

> Dönme: Reversus, converses, desertor, apostata. Der zuruck kommen ist / ein bekehrter / und ein verlaeugneter Christ. Tornato, convertito and renegar, apostat… Yehudiden ve Çıfuttan dönme. Desertor Judaicae perfidia, qui si Christianus factus est, nobis dicitur Judaeus baptısatus, aut couversus ad veram fidem Christianam, fi Mahometanus factus est, dicetur Judaeus Mahometanus factus. Ein bekehrter Jud / ein Jud der ein Lurck worden ist. Giudeo fatto Christiano, o battezato, conuertito, Giudeo fatto Turco. Juif battıse ou devenu Chrestien, Juif converti.[22]

The entry clearly suggests that the term *dönme* could mean a convert or apostate in the 17th century Ottoman cultural world. Another dictionary of the 17th–18th century, Mehmed Esad's *Lehçetü'l-Lügat*[23] has the entry for *dönme/k*, which, among other definitions, means "rucu', 'avd, dever, devran, ilhad (conversion) and irtidad (apostasy)." Likewise, the term has a strong connotation of conversion and apostasy for the Ottomans in the same century. Thus, it would not be surprising if the Turks had called the Sabbatian converts *dönme* from the very beginning of the sect.

An early 19th century Turkish-French dictionary of Kieffer and Bianchi has several entries under the root of *dönme/k*. It has a specific entry for *Dönme*, which exclusively refers to the Ottoman Sabbatians.

> Dönme: adj. et. s. t. 1. Tourné, change. 2. Apostat, renégat. *Yahudiden Dönme*. Qui a renié la foi judaique. Il existe à Salonique, une caste de ces sortes de mahométans appelés *mamin* par les Francs, et *deunme* par les Turks. Elle ne s'allie avec aucune autre caste que la sienne, et l'on croit, avec assez de fondement, qu'elle conserve et pratique secrètement son ancien culte, qui était celui des Juifs, quoiqu'elle paroisse, et par le costume, et par les noms qu'elle porte, être devenue musulmane. Son commerce principal est le tabac à fumer, et la Porte, dans ses actes, la qualifie de *Douhan tudjari thaifesi*. Communauté de merchands de tabac à fumer.[24]

---

[22] Franciscus Meninski, *Thesaurus Linguarum Orientalium TurcicaArabicae-Persica* (Vienna, 1680).

[23] Mehmed Esad Efendi, 1685-1753, *Lehcet'ul-Lugat*, haz. H. Ahmet Kırkkılıç (Ankara: TDK, 1999).

[24] J. D. Kieffer et T. X. Bianchi, *Dictionnaire Turk-Francais* (Paris, 1835).

The 19th century Ottoman dictionaries have entries for the terms *dönme* and *avdet*, which I provide here in a chronological order. Asim Efendi [Firuzabadi]'s *El-Kamus* has only the entry for *avdet*, which reads "geri dönmek, rucu' etmek, [tefsir] munsarif olduğu nesneye geri dönmek."[25] Likewise, *Muntehabat-i Lugat-i Osmaniyye* does not have an entry for *dönme/k*. Under *avdet*, it reads "çıkılan mahalle geri gelmek."[26] *Kamus-u Osmani* does not contain the word *dönme/k* but *avdet*, which reads "geri dönmek, yerine dönüp gelmek".[27]

In *Lehçe-i Osmani*, Ahmed Vefik Paşa gives a very straightforward meaning to the word *dönme*: "devr, cevelan, rucu, avdet etmek, ihtida, (conversion) irtidad, (apostasy) inkila, tersine gitmek, tahavvul."[28] In the same manner, Şemseddin Sâmi's *Kamus-u Turki* defines *dönme* as follows: "Avdet, Ricat, devr, tahvil, tagayyur, ihtida and irtidad. Dininden dönmüş (apostate), mühtedi (convert)."[29]

Ahmet Rıfat, in his dictionary *Lügat-i Tarihiyye ve Coğrafiyye*, does not have an entry for *dönme* and *avdet*, but includes a long entry for Sabbatai Sevi. Rıfat does not use any pejorative vocabulary, such as *Dönme* or *Avdeti* for the Sabbatian community, and acknowledges that Sabbatai Sevi was one of the greatest Jewish sages. After giving a very short summary of Sabbatai's adventures, he asserts the Sabbatai himself and his believers converted to Islam and were sent to settle in Salonica.[30] In time, the size of the community enlarged and it was divided into three sects: *Sazan, Honiyoz* and *Kavayeros*. Listing the names of the sub-sects was indication that the Ottomans started to notice the differences among the Sabbatian subgroups in other parts of the Empire. Among the Ottoman sources prior to this date, only Ahmed Safi who was employed in Salonica in 1873 provided the different names of the Sabbatian sub-sects. The short account by Ahmet Rıfat, flawed with factual mistakes, is the first available Ottoman narrative account of the Sabbatian movement, besides the chronicles:

> Sabbatay Hivi: He is one of the Jewish sages. He was born either in 1635 or 1640 and died in 1676. He traveled to Egypt, Turkistan, and Europe, and attained knowledge of many sciences and alchemy and rightly established fame among the people and by performing some miracles made many people servant to himself, and went to Jerusalem, and proclaimed that he was the long awaited messiah, and even attempted to proclaim his sultanate. In time,

[25] Muhammad ibn Ya'qub Firuzabadi (1329-1414), *Okyanus fi-Tercümet ül-Kamus,* 3 vols. Mütercimi Ahmet Asim Ayntabi (Kahire: Bulak Matbaasi, 1834), I, 653-4.

[26] *Müntehabat-ı Lugati Osmaniyye,* 2 vols. (Dersaadet, 1851).

[27] Mehmet Salahi (1857-1910), *Kamus-i Osmani* (İstanbul, 1895).

[28] Ahmet Vefik Paşa (1823-91), *Lehçe-i Osmâni,* hazırlayan, R. Toparli (Ankara: TDK, 2000).

[29] Şemseddin Sâmi (1850-1904), *Kâmûs-i Türki* (Istanbul: Çağrı Yayınları, 1999).

[30] Ahmet Rifat, *Lügat-i Tarihiyye ve Coğrafiyye* (Istanbul, 1882).

the Ottoman authorities realized that the Jews from Istanbul had come and joined his group, and they inspected the case and had to report about it to the Sultan who was then in Edirne. Upon the order, he was brought to the palace. While he was interrogated in the presence of the sultan, because the majesty and mercy of the sultan were involved, he and his intimate circle accepted the true religion; they were all sent to settle in Salonica. In time they increased in number, and developed three sects called *Sazan, Honiyoz* and *Kavayeros*.[31]

Since the term *dönme* could mean "to return, to convert, or to apostate," in the 17th, 18th and 19th centuries, it is reasonable to think that the Ottomans might have called the Sabbatian believers *dönme* since the inception of the community. But when the community failed to show signs of full conversion to Islam in the second and third generations, the Turks began to call them *Dönme*, with an uppercase "D." As the travelers' accounts suggest, the Ottomans already called them *Dönme* in the 18th century. On the other hand, the first available Ottoman source which contains the term *Dönme* is Ahmed Safi's treatise, entitled "*Dönmeler Adeti*" in 1873.[32]

By the second half of the 19th century, the term *Avdeti,* was added to Ottoman vocabulary and used more often to designate the sect. *Avdet* means "to go back where it once belonged or originated" in 19th century dictionaries. The shift from the term *Dönme* to *Avdeti* is hard to explain, but it seems that *Avdeti* has a more neutral or even courteous connotation than the pejorative term *Dönme*. Ottoman official documents, representing the state's attitude toward the group, preferred to use *Avdeti*, or *Avdeti Taifesi* instead of *Dönme*.[33] We find the term *Avdeti Taifesi* in the Ottoman documents, as early as in 1862.[34] Another document with regard to a mixed marriage of a Sabbatian girl and a Muslim young man, dated 1891, use the term *Avdeti*.[35] Those who did not have a negative attitude toward the Sabbatians preferred the term *Avdeti* as well. For example, Hüseyin Vassaf, in his bibliographical dictionary of the late Ottoman Sufis, *Sefine-i Evliya*, gives the family background of his teacher and famous Mesnevi commentator, Selanikli Mevlevi Esad Efendi, as someone of *Avdeti* origin.[36]

[31] Ibid., IV, 20.

[32] Ahmed Safi, *Dönmeler Adeti* (1873; reprint, ed. E. Düzdağ, Istanbul, 2001). Ahmed Safi labels them with a famous Islamic terminology "Fırka-yı zaalle" (deviated group).

[33] It is possible that this shift occurred after the *Islahat Fermani* in 1856, when the relationship between the Muslims and non-Muslims was radically reorganized, during which all negative stereotypical images about the non-Muslims were supposed to be dropped.

[34] Başbakanlık Osmanlı Arşivi, A.MKT.UM 572/1.

[35] Başbakanlık Osmanlı Arşivi, Meclisi Vükela Mazbatası 68/44.

[36] Hüseyin Vassaf (1872-1929), *Sefine-i Evliya* (Istanbul, 1990), I, 329, writes: "He was my spiritual mentor and was born in 1843 into the family of Receb Efendi the *avdeti*, who was a merchant in Salonica."

Based on this twist in the Ottoman vocabulary, we can assume that the crypto life of the Sabbatians became clearer to the outside society, and that knowledge of it traveled to other cities of the Ottoman Empire in the 19th century. The group was then labeled as *Avdeti*—that is, "someone who returned to his origins." *Dönme* and *Avdeti* were mostly used interchangeably by the Ottomans until the twentieth century when the term *Selanikli* was added to the plethora of designations; that last became increasingly common during the time of Turkish Republic.

The suggestion that the Turks did not call the Sabbatian converts exclusively *Dönme* in the first generation is further corroborated by foreign observers. On the existence of the Sabbatian community in Salonica, the first available source is a letter from a French missionary in Salonica of the 1730s. The missionary Jean-Baptiste Souciet calls them "new Muslims," without referring to them as *Ma'amin* or *Dönme*.

> Les nouveaux musulmans, originairement juifs, sont peu estimés des anciens mahométans; ils conservent toujours de père en fils une inclination secrète pour le judaïsme, jusqu'á réciter leurs anciennes prières au lieu de celles du Coran.[37]

James Porter, writing in 1768, almost 90 years after the establishment of the community, gives us no hint as to what the Sabbatian community was called. Porter reports that the believers established a distinct crypto community in Salonica. He was puzzled by the fact that the Turks did not recognize their secret life. He adds that although the Turks may have known about it, the cosmopolitanism of Turkish culture would have allowed for the existence of sectarian life.

> There is however, one sect in Turkey, principally at Salonica of very particular kind, it has sprung from one Sabbatai Sevi.. .They profess publicly the Mahometan religion, and retain privately the Jewish rites, much on the principle of the Ebionites, among the first Christians: they intermarry, inhabit together in the same part of the town, and never mix with Mahometans, except on business and commerce, or in the mosches . . . though were these Jewish Mahometans publicly to profess both, they would be instantly made a public example: death is the doom of an apostate.[38]

Admitting that he never saw a *Dönme* himself, Carsten Niebuhr gathered information from different people including a certain rabbi from Constantinople. He reports that there were at Salonica about 600 families of that sect, generally known by the name *Dolmäh,* only associating amongst themselves and not intermarrying with others.

Daselbst findet man wohl 600 Familien, die sich zu ihrer Religion beken-

---

[37] Souciet, "De la ville Salonique," 78-79.

[38] Sir James Porter (1710-76), *Observations on the religion, law, government, and manners, of the Turks* (London, 1768), II, 40-41.

nen, und als solche unter dem Namen Dolmäh, b. h. Abtrünnige, so wohl bet Mohammedanern als Juden und Christen bekant sind.[39]

Niebuhr translates the word *Dönme* with negative connotations, as "Abtrünnige," i.e. renegade; deserter; apostate (from religion or sect); turncoat. Peter Beer and subsequently M. Mayers seem to borrow the term *Dolmach* from Niebuhr in describing the Sabbatian community in the 1820s. Most of Beer's information, and hence that of Mayers' about the Sabbatians is a replica of Niebuhr.[40] However both Beer and Mayer call them also "Zohariten."

Writing in 1777, J. V. Arasy, a longtime French ambassador to Salonica, estimating their numbers to be about five thousand, and he refers to the Ottoman Sabbatians as "*mamins*," as the believers called themselves.

> On compte à pue près soixante et dix mille habitant à Salonique, dont trente mille Turcs, vingt cinq mille Juifs et quinze mille Grecs. Parmi les premiers il y en a cinq mille environ, connus sous le nom de *mamins*.[41]

In 1804, W. M. Leake still calls them *mamins*. Interestingly, all of the observers seem to have a strong opinion that the *Dönmes* were practicing some Jewish rites and rituals. It seems that they could not penetrate the differences and peculiarities of the Sabbatian theology, which was in fact a mixture of Jewish and Islamic beliefs and practices.

> A considerable portion of [the Jews] have become Musulmans since that time, though without being altogether acknowledged by the *Osmanlis*, and forming a separate class under the denomination of *Mamins*.[42]

Esprit Cousinéry, who was another French ambassador to Salonica around the turn of the 19th century, used the term *Dunme* in his account. It is easy to assume that he read the account of his predecessor, Arasy, but he did not refer to them as *mamins*.

> Il se trouve dans la même ville un grand nombre d'autres Juifs qui se sont faits Turcs en apparence, mais qui, dit-on, pratiquent toujours la religion de Moïse. C'est pourquoi on leur a donné le nom de *Dunme* ou de *faux apostats*.[43]

Visiting the city in 1826, a missionary of the British and Foreign Bible Soci-

---

[39] Niebuhr, "Von Vershidenen Nationen." There is a confusion as to when the article appeared. Peter Beer gives the date of the article as 1784, whereas Graetz gives it as 1774. Apparently Niebuhr visited Salonica in 1774 but wrote his article in 1784.

[40] P. Beer, *Religiosen Sekten der Juden*, 259, 294; M. Mayers, *A Brief Account of the Zoharite Jews* (Cambridge, 1826).

[41] J.V. Arasy, "Description Des Pays du department du consulat de Salonique," 17-18.

[42] Leake, *Travels in Northern Greece*, III, 250.

[43] E. Cousinéry, *Voyage dans la Macédoine* (Paris, 1831) II, 19-20.

ety,[44] Benjamin Barker, gathered information about the Jews and the *Dönmes*, and prepared a report about them. Thinking that they were 1200 souls altogether in Salonica, Barker is the first one to talk about the Sabbatian sub-sects:

> The Jewish-Turks are a sect whom, I have never heard mentioned before, although they tell me that some of them exist at Constantinople...They are called by the Turkish *Donmethes*, or renegados, and are divided in three separate classes; viz. *Bezestenlithes, Ghoniothes, and Cavalieros*. Each class is distinct, as they do not intermarry, nor have they any kind of connexion one with the other, or with the Turks. It is generally supposed that they still retain many of their Jewish ceremonies and observances, and many think that in secret they are still Jews... It is the firm opinion of many, that they are only Turks externally, in order that they may enjoy the same privilege with them.[45]

American missionaries developed a deep interest in the *Dönmes* as well.[46] Josiah Brewer was the first American missionary who reported about the existence of the *Dönmes* (*Donmethes* or Renegados) in Salonica in 1827. It seems that the American missionary board owes their first information about the *Dönmes* to the English missionary activities in Salonica, since Brewer repeats almost verbatim what Barker wrote about them.[47] Edward M. Dodd, who was another American missionary to the Jews in Salonica in 1849, mentions that the Jews also contemptuously called them *Dunmehs* (turncoats).[48]

Since the community was relatively closed to the outside world in the 18th century, available sources before the 19th century did not recognize the existence of the sub-sects and referred to them as a monolithic *Dönme* community. As the community was exposed to outsiders, however, the sub-sects began to be

[44] During the 19th century, the British and Foreign Bible Society, then the American Board of Commissioners for Foreign Missions (ABCFM), and then the Scottish Bible Society sent many missionaries to Salonica and prepared reports about the religious composition of the city. Most of them exclusively targeted the Jews and Dönmes.

[45] "Extracts from Mr. Barker's Journal," *Twenty-third Report of British and Foreign Bible Society*, 1827, with an Appendix (London, 1827), 79.

[46] About a short history of the American mission among the Jews in the East, see Charles Troubridge Riggs, *History of the Works in the Near East and more especially in Turkey, 1819-1934*. ABCFM manuscript histories of missions, from Brown accord Case Row C22/3rd Case/4th row, 20-25: "The first missionary sent by the Board to the Jews in the Levant, was the Rev. Josiah Brewer, who, while connected with the Board, was supported by the 'Female Society of Boston and Vicinity for Promoting Christianity among the Jews.' ... After the retirement of Mr. Brewer, the ladies assumed the support of the Rev. William G. Schauffler, who became his successor."

[47] J. Brewer, *A Residence at Constantinople in the Year 1827* (New Haven, 1830), 293-94.

[48] Edward Dodd, "Mission to the Jews," in *40th Annual Report of the American Board of Commissioners for Foreign Missions* (Boston, 1849), 106.

recognized. Although the *Dönme* sub-sects came to be known *Yakubis, Karakaş,* and *Kapancılar* in the 20th century thanks to the works of Abraham Galante,[49] the sub-sects were known by different designations in the 19th and early 20th centuries. As noted, the earliest available record, referring to the subgroups belongs to the British missionary Benjamin Barker, who designates them as *Bezestenlithes, Ghonlothes,* and *Cavalieros* in 1827.[50]

The first available Turkish source, dated 1873, belongs to Ahmed Safi, who categorizes the Sabbatians as "Terpuş, Karu (İstanbullu dahi derler)" and "Honyoz (Çorapçı dahi derler)."[51] The other early Turkish source that was aware of the existence of the subgroups was the dictionary of Ahmet Rıfat, dated 1882, which designates the groups as *Sazan, Honiyoz and Kavayeros.*[52] Another report from the 19th and the beginning of the 20th centuries speaks of *Izmirlis* or *Kavalieros, Jakubis,* and *Koniosos.*[53]

Although not dated, there are many other names for the subgroups. The *Yakubiler* are also called *Arpados* [clean-shaven], *Tarbuşlis* and *Hamdi Beyler.* The *Karakaşlar* are also called *Mu'minler, Osman Babalar, On Yollular, Honiyozlar, Coniozos, Koniososlar,* and *Konyosos.* Likewise the *Kapancılar* are also called *Papular (kidemli eski), Ibrahim Ağalılar, Cavalieros, Kavalieoros, Izmirliler* and *Cavaglieros.*[54] Table 1 lists all the different names of the Sabbatians, as they appeared in available texts that belonged to the different time periods:

---

[49] Abraham Galante, *Nouveaux Documents sur Sabbetai Sevi: Organisation et us et Coutumes de ses Adeptes* (Istanbul, 1935).

[50] Barker, *Twenty-third Report,* 79.

[51] Ahmed Safi, *Dönmeler Adeti,* 43.

[52] Ahmet Rifat, *Lügat-i Tarihiyye ve Coğrafiyye,* IV, 20.

[53] Cited in Gershom Scholem, "The Crypto-Jewish Sect of the Dönmeh (Sabbatians) in Turkey," in *Messianic Idea in Judaism* (New York: Socken, 1971), 142-167.

[54] Cited in Ben Zwi, *The Exiled and the Redeemed,* 116-120.

Table 1. *The Many Names for the Sabbatians.*

SABBATIANS
Dönmeler
Avdetiler
Selanikliler
Pastelikos
Sabetaycılar
Minim
Ma'miniko
Ma'amin
Haverim
Mamzerim
Ba'ale Milhama
Patrones de la pelea
Zoharites
Dolmethes
Mohemmedan Jews
Jew-Turks
Turkish-Jews
Zabbathaites

Table 2. *The Subgroups and Their Other Names.*

YAKUBILER	KARAKAŞLAR	KAPANCILAR
Jakubis	Osman Babalar,	Papular
Arpados	On Yollular	Ibrahim Ağalar
Tarbushlis	Honiyozlar	Çelebiler
Hamdi Beyler	Coniozos	Cavalieros
Sazan	Koniososlar	Kavalieoros
Bezestenlithes	Konyosos	Cavaglieros
	Omoscos	Izmirliler
	Honyoz	Karu
	Çorapçılar	Istanbullular
	Basık Burunlar	Onculer
	Berberi	Traschi
	Komflu Ağaları	
	Ghoniothes	

To conclude, Turkish Muslims, Jews, Western observers, and the Sabbatians themselves perceived their group differently and call the Sabbatians by various names. The terms *mühtedi, nevmüslim,* or *dönme* were used to identify the first generation of the Sabbatian converts—that is, assuming that they were regular converts. Although those terms were supposed to be dropped in the second and third generation, as was the case of other converts, outsiders continued to use the term *Dönme* with a connotation of crypto belief and practices, and this term appears already in the 18th century. Both the designations *Dönme* and *Avdeti* denoted that there was something different and even unacceptable about those new Muslims. By those terms, the larger Muslim community probably wanted to refer to their conversion as an incomplete process, positioning the Sabbatians in a liminal state.

Although the Sabbatian called themselves believers, implying that they were believing in a unique Sabbatian theology, the Jews called them heretics, and Western observers referred to them as "secret Jews." These designations continued until 1924, when the traditional structure of the Sabbatian communities was dismantled and they were diffused and incorporated into the population of the new Turkish Republic.*

*Part of this study was undertaken as an ARIT-NEH Fellow in Turkey in 2004-2005.

View across the Golden Horn, ca. 1875, photograph by Pascal Sébah used as a postcard by Römmler and Jonas of Dresden (collection of Nezih Başgelen, Istanbul).

4

THE 1829 CENSUS AND ISTANBUL'S POPULATION DURING THE LATE 18TH AND EARLY 19TH CENTURIES

BETÜL BAŞARAN

Ottoman lands attracted newcomers from various regions and for a variety of reasons, including conquest and warfare, as well as political, ethno-religious, and economic factors.* During the 18th and 19th centuries there were both mass migration and chain migration movements toward Istanbul. Mass migrations brought flocks of predominantly Muslim refugees, often as a result of the frequent political border changes that occurred during the 19th century.[1] Along with the politically motivated massive waves of migration, however, Istanbul also attracted an uncontrollable flow of rural migrants in search of work and socioeconomic opportunities.[2] In addition to merchants, craftsmen, *medrese*

* This chapter is part of a larger project on Istanbul's population and various registers dating from the late 18th and early 19th centuries. For a discussion of these registers see my "Remaking the Gate of Felicity: Policing, Social Control, and Migration in Istanbul at the end of the Eighteenth Century, 1789-1793" (Ph.D. dissertation, University of Chicago, 2006).

[1] The best example of the political mass migrations in the 18th century is the influx of Crimean Tatars into the Ottoman Empire following Russia's annexation of Crimea in 1783–84. For 18th century population movements see Bruce McGowan, "The Age of the Ayans, 1699–1812," in H. İnalcik and D. Quataert, eds., *A Social and Economic History of the Ottoman Empire. Volume Two, 1600–1914* (Cambridge: Cambridge University Press, 1997), 646–50. For different estimates and a detailed account of external migrations in the 19th century see Ahmet Akgündüz, "Osmanlı İmparatorluğu ve Dış Göçler, 1782–1922," *Toplum ve Bilim* 80 (1999): 144–70, and McGowan, "Age of the Ayans," 793–95. A turning point came in 1857 with the Law of Immigrants (*Muhācirūn Kanunnāmesi*), after which the Ottoman Empire officially began to accept and encourage external migrations and granted immigrants tax exemptions as well as exemption from military service and religious freedom. One could argue that the reason behind these changes was compensation for the population decrease and the agricultural losses that resulted from wars, high taxes, epidemics, and inefficient management; see Kemal Karpat, *Ottoman Population 1830–1914: Demographic and Social Characteristics* (Madison, WI: University of Wisconsin Press, 1985).

[2] Cem Behar, *A Neighborhood in Ottoman Istanbul: Fruit Vendors and Civil Servants in the Kasap İlyas Mahalle* (Albany, NY: SUNY Press, 2003), 95.

students, dervishes, and beggars, the influx of young men (*bīkārān*) and house-holds (*ev göçü* or *harem göçü*) seem to have been common during the 18th cen-tury. Life was presumably more secure in the capital city, and there were large numbers of religious foundations and hospices that regularly fed the poor. İnalcık wrote that the hospice of Fatih alone fed a thousand people each day.[3] According to one estimate, in the second half on the 17th century there were 485 mosques, 4492 *mescids*, 157 *tekkes* and 385 *zaviyes* in Istanbul.[4] As Cem Behar put it, "uncontrolled migration to Istanbul was always a politically sensitive issue, and migrants were perceived, first and foremost, as a potential threat to political stability in the sensitive and 'protected' imperial capital. Uprisings and various real or imaginary urban disorders, 'of a physical as well as a moral sort' were often attributed to the presence of uncontrolled elements in the capital, and especially of groups of provincial and unsettled younger males who came seeking employment."[5]

Ottoman sources and documents from the 18th century address the issue of migration on a broad and indiscriminate level and make no distinction between the different types of immigrants. People came to the capital city for various purposes and different lengths of time—for long-term residence, as annual or temporary workers, or temporary sojourners, bringing petitions to submit to the court or goods to be delivered. In most cases it is not possible to distinguish between seasonal migrants and potentially permanent immigrants in the court records or in the imperial orders drafted by Ottoman administrators.[6] More-over, it is difficult at the current state of scholarship to determine whether these movements led to an actual increase in the city's population or not. It is proba-ble that newcomers quickly replaced those who died as a result of epidemics, earthquakes, and fires in the city. The integration of the migrants into the life of the city depended on complicated occupational and regional networks. People could come and stay for a while, then rent their shops and tools temporarily or permanently, or they could return to their place of origin or seek their fortune in another town. Such dynamics as these most likely depended on what other towns or cities had to offer in terms of economic and social opportunities com-pared to life in Istanbul, especially during a troubled period when the cost of internal and external wars intensified the economic problems of the empire, as well as difficulties associated with the provisioning of the city.

[3] "Istanbul," *Encyclopaedia of Islam* (Leiden: Brill, 1999), CD-Rom version.

[4] Robert Mantran, *Istanbul dans la second moitié du XVII siècle, Essai d'histoire institu-tionelle, économique et sociale* (Paris: Librarie Adrien Maisonneuve, 1962), 110.

[5] Behar, *Neighborhood*, 96.

[6] Suraiya Faroqhi, "Migration into Eighteenth-Century Greater Istanbul as Reflected in the Kadı Registers of Eyüp," *Turcica* 30 (1998): 163–83, esp. p. 169.

ISTANBUL'S POPULATION
AT THE TURN OF THE 19TH CENTURY

There are no reliable estimates on the population of the greater Istanbul area, including the three townships of Eyüp, Galata, and Üsküdar, before the 19th century. The first attempt at an empire-wide census took place in 1830–31 in order to determine the number of men eligible for military service after the abolition of the Janissary corps in 1826. This census did not include females, and its figures are available only for parts of the empire.[7] Even before the census of 1831, however, there were a number of attempts between 1828 and 1830 to obtain reliable figures for the number of males in Istanbul, again primarily for military purposes.[8] In the fall of 1829, while peace with Russia was being negotiated, a census of the male population of the city, including infants, was already under way.[9] The census started with a count of Muslim males, and then proceeded with non-Muslims. The estimates from this census are not available for inner Istanbul, however, but only for eight neighborhoods within the township of Galata. The census register (*müfredāt defteri*) includes physical descriptions, occupations, and geographical origins of 1,156 Muslim males, and by comparison to earlier registers and the 1830–31 census, it deserves recognition as a modern census preceding that of 1831.[10]

The focus of this chapter is another, earlier census mentioned by the court historian Ahmed Lūtfī Efendi. During the winter of 1829, there was a severe shortage of grain supplies in Istanbul as a result of the ongoing war with Russia, compounded by the loss of expected grain shipments from the Black Sea. Lūtfī describes in detail the poor quality of bread in the markets and unrest among the people, and explains that in order to determine the exact number of people in the city who needed bread, census registers were compiled in Istanbul and the three adjoining townships.[11] The judge of Istanbul received an imperial order on February 2, 1829 (H. 5 Şevval 1244), instructing him to work with the market inspector (*ihtisāb ağası*) to produce a register of every person, Muslim and non-Muslim, in residential neighborhoods and inns, so that appropriate amounts of

---

[7] See Karpat, *Ottoman Population*. The census of 1831 is known as the first Ottoman census in the modern sense since the publication of Enver Ziya Karal's work under the title "The First Population Census in the Ottoman Empire" in 1943; see Enver Ziya Karal, *Osmanlı İmparatorluğu'nda İlk Nüfus Sayımı, 1831* (Ankara: Basım ve Ciltevi, 1943).

[8] See Sedat Bingöl, *1829 İstanbul Nüfus Sayımı ve Tophane Kasabası* (Eskişehir: Anadolu Üniversitesi Edebiyat Fakültesi Yayınları, 2004).

[9] Başbakanlık Osmanlı Arşivi [BOA] Hatt-ı Hümayun Tasnifi [HH] 19270.

[10] The register is transliterated in its entirety in Bingöl, *1829 İstanbul*.

[11] "*Zuhūr-ı emāre-i kaht der-İstanbul.*" –Ahmed Lūtfī Efendi, *Vak'anüvīs Ahmed Lūtfī Efendi Tarihi*, trans. (from Ottoman to Modern Turkish) Yücel Demirel and Tamer Erdoğan (Istanbul: YKY, 1999), II, 361–62.

bread could be rationed on a daily basis.[12] We understand from this document that the government was concerned with people buying more bread than they needed in order to save some for emergencies, thus aggravating scarcity and causing the gathering of angry mobs in front of bakeries. All neighborhood imams, the Greek and Armenian patriarchs, and the chief Rabbi of Istanbul received orders requiring them to send to the judge the exact number of people in their communities. The imperial orders in the court records and Lūtfī Efendi's chronicle suggest that the judge of Istanbul received some estimates from the leaders of Muslim and non-Muslim communities in a fairly short period of time and drafted registers for each region based on these estimates.

According to Lūtfī Efendi, these registers yielded a total of 359,089 people in the greater Istanbul area.[13] To the best of my knowledge, no estimates from these registers have previously been published. During my research in the Ottoman archives, I was fortunate enough to locate the census register for inner Istanbul. This census includes a list of 287 neighborhoods and the total number of Muslims (male and female) in each neighborhood, including students of theological seminaries (*medrese*), Gypsies (*tā'ife-i kıptiyān*), and bachelors (Muslim and non-Muslim) residing in various inns (compare Tables 1–3). The total Muslim population of inner Istanbul in this register is just under 94,000. With the addition of the number of Muslim and non-Muslim bachelors, the total rises to about 100,000 people (Tables 1, 2).[14] Whereas the censuses of 1829–31 were conducted for military purposes and included males only, the 1829 census register for inner Istanbul includes females as well. The documents clearly state that every person was to be counted precisely (*her hānede mevcūd ehl-i İslāmdan ne mikdār nüfūs var ise; . . . ve bir hānede ehl-i İslāmdan kaç cān var ise ziyāde haber verilmeyüb*).[15]

[12] İstanbul Mahkemesi [IM] (Court Records of Istanbul) 154: 70–71.

[13] Ahmed Lūtfī Efendi, *Vak'anüvīs*, II, 361.

[14] Bab-ı Asafi Divan Beylikçi Kalemi- Mühimme [A. DVN. MHM.] 972 (9 Şevval 1244/April 14, 1829).   [15] IM 154: 70.

Table 1. *Population of Inner Istanbul in 1829.*

SUBDIVISIONS (ĶOL)	NUMBER OF NEIGHBORHOODS	NUMBER OF MUSLIMS
Çarşı ķolu	32*	7,583
Cibāli ķolu	55	21,589
Balat ķolu	63	21,494
Kumķapı ķolu	58	19,349
Yediķule ķolu	32	11,513
Topķapı ķolu	47	12,465
TOTAL	287	93,993

Source: A. DVN. MHM. 972.
* Two neighborhoods in Çarşı kolu were recorded as one, so the total number of neighborhoods was actually 288.

Table 2. *Bachelors in Inner Istanbul in 1829.*

Muslim	1,823
Non-Muslim	4,262
TOTAL	6,085

Source: A. DVN. MHM. 972.

Table 3. *Population of Inner Istanbul in 1830.*

SUBDIVISIONS (ĶOL)	NUMBER OF NEIGHBORHOODS	NUMBER OF MUSLIM MALES
Çarşı ķolu	32	7,135
Cibāli ķolu	56	9,446
Balat ķolu	62	10,120
Kumķapı ķolu	58	10,372
Yediķule ķolu	33	5,148
Topķapı ķolu	47	5,002
TOTAL	288	47,223

Source: Kemal Karpat, *Ottoman Population 1830–1914* (Madison, WI: University of Wisconsin Press, 1985), 202.
* The distribution of neighborhoods appears to have changed slightly compared to the 1829 census register (Table 1).

Table 4. *Muslim Inn Dwellers/Bachelors in Greater Istanbul in 1830.*

Strong *(tuvānā)**	3,375
Infants *(sabī)*†	20
Old *(müsin)*§	1,602
TOTAL	4,997

Source: Kemal Karpat, *Ottoman Population 1830–1914* (Madison, WI: University of Wisconsin Press, 1985), 202.

* Generally 18-50 years of age   † Presumably orphans   § Older than 50 years of age

How can these figures help us produce realistic population estimates for the late 18th century? Available figures for the population of greater Istanbul during the 18th century vary widely from 400,000 to 1,000,000.[16] These figures are not based on official sources, and they comprise, for the most part, the observations of Western travelers who visited the city. Among them, for example, is the French traveler Guillaume-Antoine Olivier, who estimated the population of greater Istanbul in 1792 to be around 500,000 people based on the daily grain consumption in the city's bread bakeries.[17] Following the example of Olivier, William Eton attempted to calculate the population of Istanbul in 1798, based on the daily grain consumption, and arrived at an estimate of 426,000 people, with no more

[16] Compare Charles Issawi, "Population and Resources in the Ottoman Empire and Iran," in R. Owen and G. Naff, eds., *Studies in Eighteenth Century Islamic History* (Carbondale, IL: Southern Illinois University Press, 1977), 152–53; Donald Quataert, *The Ottoman Empire 1700–1922* (Cambridge: Cambridge University Press, 2000), 210–16; Stanford Shaw, "The Population of Istanbul in the Nineteenth Century," *IJMES* 10 (1979): 265–77; Cem Behar, *The Population of the Ottoman Empire and Turkey, 1500–1927* (Ankara: State Institute of Statistics, 1996); Cem Behar, "Osmanlı Nüfus İstatistikleri ve 1831 Sonrası Modernleşmesi," in Halil İnalcık and Şevket Pamuk, eds., *Osmanlı Devletinde Bilgi ve İstatistik [Data and Statistics in the Ottoman Empire]* (Ankara: T. C. Başbakanlık İstatistik Enstitüsü, 2000), 63–72. See also Zafer Toprak, "Tarihsel Nüfusbilim Açısından İstanbul'un Nüfusu ve Toplumsal Topoğrafyası," *Toplum ve Ekonomi* 3 (April 1992): 109–20; Zafer Toprak, "Nüfus: Fetihten 1950'ye," *Dünden Bugüne İstanbul Ansiklopedisi* (Ankara: Kültür Bakanlığı, 1993), VI, 108–11; Selim Deringil, "19. Yüzyılda Osmanlı İmparatorluğu'na Göç Olgusu Üzerine Bazı Düşünceler," in Mübahat Kütükoğlu, ed., *Prof. Dr. Bekir Kütükoğlu'na Armağan* (Istanbul: Edebiyat Fakültesi Yayınları, 1991), 435–42; Rukiye Bulut, "18. yüzyılda İstanbul nüfusunun artmaması için alınan tedbirler," *Belgelerle Türk Tarihi Dergisi* 3 (Aralık/December 1967): 30–32.

[17] Guillaume-Antoine Olivier, *Voyage dans l'Empire Ottoman, l'Egypte et la Perse* (Paris: Agasse, 1809); see also Engin Deniz Akarlı, "Ottoman Population in Europe in the 19th Century: Its Territorial, Racial and Religious Composition" (Master's thesis, University of Wisconsin, 1972). Cem Behar and Kemal Karpat both made use of Akarlı's estimates in their works. See Behar, *Neighborhood*, and Karpat, *Ottoman Population*.

than 300,000 permanent inhabitants.[18] According to McGowan, the old city within the walls may have held around 300–350,000 inhabitants when not devastated by fire or epidemic, and the total population, including suburbs, was about 600,000 in the late 18th century.[19] In light of the available estimates from 1829, the upper limit of these estimates appears to be exaggerated.

In the absence of reliable figures for the 18th century, if we apply the 58:42 ratio of Muslims to non-Muslims in inner Istanbul[20] to the 100,000 figure (the total from Tables 1 and 2), which included Muslims and bachelors in the bread census, we arrive at roughly 71,200 non-Muslims, a figure which then yields a total population of 171,200 people for inner Istanbul in 1829. This number includes inn dwellers/bachelors, but does not take into account other groups residing in the city, such as the residents of the Topkapı palace, the residents of the palaces of female members of the royal family and various dignitaries, soldiers in military barracks, and foreigners (mostly in Galata/Pera). Based on this partially reliable data, then, one could hypothesize that the population of inner Istanbul was not more than 200,000 at the end of the 18th century.

A comparison of the estimated number of people in inner Istanbul (171,200) and Lūtfī's estimate for greater Istanbul in 1829 (360,000) yields to a ratio of 47.6 to 52.4. If we apply this ratio to the 200,000 estimate for inner Istanbul at the end of the 18th century, we get roughly 420,168 people in the greater Istanbul area for that period. This rough estimate is in fact quite close to Eton's calculations for 1798 (426,000 people).

In conclusion, although it may be impossible to produce completely reliable numbers, the available data, taken together, suggest that only the lower end of the estimates ranging from 400,000 to 1,000,000 people would seem to be realistic for the population at the turn of the 19th century in the greater Istanbul area.

[18] William Eton, *A Survey of the Turkish Empire* (London: T. Cadell, Jun. and W. Davies, 1798), 282 (rpt. New York: Arno Press, 1973). On Istanbul's grain and particularly its bread consumption see Lynne Marie Thornton Sasmazer, "Provisioning Istanbul: Bread Production, Power and Political Ideology in the Ottoman Empire, 1789–1807" (Ph.D. dissertation, Indiana University, 2000).

[19] McGowan, *Age of the Ayans*, 652; based on Issawi, "Population and Resources," 152; and "Istanbul," *Encyclopaedia of Islam* (Leiden: Brill, 1999), CD-Rom version.

[20] This ratio represents roughly the average of three separate estimates for the 16th and 17th centuries. The first is provided by Sinan Paşa's private physician Cristobal, who estimated 60,000 Muslim households and 44,000 non-Muslim households around 1550, which yields a ratio of 57.7 : 42.3; see Robert Mantran, *La vie quotidienne à Istanbul au siècle de Soliman le Magnifique* (Paris: Hachette, 1990), 45. The second estimate is 46,635 Muslim households and 33,362 non-Muslim ones with a ratio of 58.3 : 41.7 between 1520 and 1535: Ömer Lütfi Barkan, "Essai sur les données statistique des registres de recensement dans l'Empire ottoman aux XVe et XVIe siècles." *JESHO* 1 (August 1957): 20. The third comes from correspondence from Fabre, a French merchant in Istanbul, who estimated about 2,000 Muslim and 1,397 non-Muslim households, a much lower estimate compared to the first two, but nevertheless yielding almost the same ratio of 58.8 : 41.2; Mantran, *Vie quotidienne*, 47.

Table 5. *Population of Greater Istanbul in 1829.*

	*Muslims & bachelors**	*Non-Muslims based on 58:42 ratio†*	TOTAL	%
Inner Istanbul	100,000	71,200	171,200	47.6%
Bilād-ı şelāşe	-	-	188,800	52.4%
Greater Istanbul	-	-	360,000	100%

Source: A. DVN. MHM 972 and Ahmed Lūtfī Efendi
* Bachelors include Muslim and non-Muslims   † See note 20

Table 6. *Estimated Population of Greater Istanbul at the End of the 18th Century based on 1829 ratios.*

	Muslims & Non-Muslims	%
Inner Istanbul	≤ 200,000	47.6%
Bilād-ı şelāşe	≤ 220,168	52.4%
Greater Istanbul	≤ 420,168	100%

Source: Based on percentage values from Table 5

The Neighborhoods of Inner Istanbul in the Six Subdivisions in 1829
A. DVN. MHM 972 (H. 1244)

The numbers that appear in brackets before each entry most likely refer to the branches for the bread makers (*fırıncı esnafına ait kol sayıları*). In his book on the bakeries and mills on Istanbul, Aynural mentions that there were 61 such branches at the end of the 18th century. The numbers in the register range from 1 to 62. See Salih Aynural, *İstanbul Değirmenleri ve Fırınları. Zahire Ticareti* (İstanbul: Tarih Vakfı Yurt Yayınları, 2001), 120.

The numbers that appear at the end of each entry reflect the number of persons recorded in that neighborhood. Some entries include the number of students and employees in religious seminaries, as well as Gypsies.

Āsitāne-i 'aliyyede kāin bi'l-cümle mahallet altı kol i'tibārıyla

EVVELKİ ÇARŞI KOLU

[3] Bāb-i 'Ālī civārında Lālā Hayreddin Mahallesi; nüfūs: 285
[3] Hoca Paşa civārında Hobyār Mahallesi; nüfūs: 562
[3] Hoca Paşa civārında Karakī Hüseyin Çelebi Mahallesi; nüfūs: 452
[3] Hoca Paşa kurbunda Elvānzāde Mahallesi;
Nüfūs: 460
            <u>001</u> (Bostancıbaşı medresesinde sākin talebeden)
            461
[3] Hoca Paşa Mahallesi;
Nüfūs: 297
            <u>009</u> [Sultān 'Abdülhamīd Hān hazretleri medresesinde mevcūd
   talebeden]
            306
[3] Hoca Paşa kurbunda Sahhāf Süleymān Mahallesi; nüfūs: 15
[3] Hoca Paşa kurbunda Nallı Mescīd nām-ı diğer İmām 'Ali Mahallesi; nüfūs: 116
[3] Uzun Çarşı başında İbrāhīm Paşa-yı 'Atīk Mahallesi; nüfūs: 332
[4] Uzun Çarşı kurbunda Bazār-ı cedid Mahallesi; nüfūs: 261
(Civārında Molla Gürānī Mahallesi ahālisi kalīl olmağla ilhāken tahrīr olunmuştur)
[4] Uzun Çarşı civārında Samanviren-i evvel Mahallesi; nüfūs:371
[4] Uzun Çarşı civārında Samanviren-i sānī Mahallesi; nüfūs: 161
[4] Uzun Çarşı civārında Yavaşça Şahin Mahallesi; nüfūs: 155
[4] Çarşı-yı kebīr kurbunda Mahmūd Paşa Mahallesi
Nüfūs: 296
            <u>020</u> [ketebe-i mahkeme-i Mahmūd Paşa]
            316
            <u>004</u> [Nūr-i Osmānī medresesinde sākin talebeden]
            320
[4] Mahmūd Paşa civārinda Hācı Küçük[?] Mahallesi; nüfūs: 260
[4] Mahmūd Paşa kurbunda Dāye Hātūn Mahallesi; nüfūs: 142
[4] Mahmūd Paşa kurbunda Tarakcılar civārında Dāye Hātūn Mahallesi
Nüfūs: 211

[4] Mahmūd Paşa civārında Hoca Kāsım Ağa Mahallesi; nüfūs: 46
[7] Cağalazāde meydanı kurbunda Cezerī Kāsım Paşa Mahallesi; nüfūs: 276
[48] Irgāt pazarı kurbunda Kaliçeci Hasan Mahallesi; nüfūs: 119
[48] Irgat pazarı civārında Molla Hayreddin Mahallesi; nüfūs: 61
[48] Sultān Bāyezīd-i Veli Han Mahallesi
Nüfūs:　　　　　460
　　　　　　　　002 [Cedide Esseyyid Hasan Paşa medresesinde sākin talebeden]
　　　　　　　　462
　　　　　　　　008 [Sultān Bāyezīd medresesi]
　　　　　　　　470
[48] Bab-ı hazret-i seraskeri civārında Mercan Ağa Mahallesi; nüfūs: 437
[48] Tavuk pazarı civārında Hüseyin Ağa Mahallesi; nüfūs: 87
[48] Fazıl Paşa kurbunda Hoca Ferhad nām-ı diğerAsmalı Mescid Mahallesi
Nüfūs:　　　　　14
[48] Sedefciler kurbunda Gazi 'Atīk Ali Paşa Mahallesi; nüfūs: 187
[7] Demirkapı civārında Dāye Hātūn Mahallesi; nüfūs: 325
[8] Alaca Hamām kurbunda Çelebioğlu 'Alāaddin Mahallesi
Nüfūs:　　　　　591
　　　　　　　　002 [Vālide Sultān Dārü'l-hadīs medresesinde sākin talebeden]
　　　　　　　　593
[7] Acı Hamām kurbunda Asmalı Mescīd civārında Hoca Rüstem Mahallesi
Nüfūs:　　　　　133

[8] Āhī Çelebi Mahallesi; nüfūs: 33
[8] Kapan-ı 'Asel civārında Rüstem Paşa Mahallesi;nüfūs: 60
[5] Bāğçekapısı civārında Şeyh Mehmed Geylānī Mahallesi; nüfūs: 332

KUMKAPI KOLU

[58] Sultān Ahmed civārında Sinān Ağa nām-ı diğer Kabasakal Mahallesi
Nüfūs:　　　　　993
[58] Sultān Ahmed civārında Helvacıbaşı İskender Ağa Mahallesi; nüfūs: 92
[58] Sultān Ahmed kurbunda Güngörmez Mahallesi; nüfūs: 320
[58] Sultān Ahmed kurbunda Üçler Mahallesi; nüfūs: 378
[58] Sultān Ahmed kurbunda Firūz Ağa Mahallesi; nüfūs: 488
[58] Sultān Ahmed kurbunda Nahılbend Hācı Hasan Ağa Mahallesi; nüfūs: 802
[59] Āhurkapı civārında Kapıağası Mahmūd Ağa Mahallesi; nüfūs: 350
[59] Āhurkapı civārında Akbıyık Mahallesi; nüfūs: 756
[59] Küçük Ayasofya Mahallesi; nüfūs: 1342
[61] Kadırga Limanı kurbunda Şehsüvār Mahallesi; nüfūs: 296
[61] Kadırga Limanı kurbunda Akar Çeşme civārında Emīn Sinān Mahallesi
Nüfūs:　　　　　218
[59] Āhurkapı civārında Seyyid Hasan nām-ı diğer Cankurtaran Mahallesi
Nüfūs:　　　　　220
[59] Āhurkapı civārında İshāk Paşa Mahallesi; nüfūs: 789
[61] Kadırga Limanı kurbunda Kātib Sinān Mahallesi; nüfūs: 51
[61] Kadırga Limanı kurbunda Bostan Mahallesi; nüfūs: 301
[59] Peykhāne kurbunda Uzun Şecā'addin Mahallesi; nüfūs: 127
[59] Uzun Şecā'addin Mahallesine mülhak kule bostanında Sinān Ağa Mahallesi
Nüfūs:　　　　　31
[7] Gedik Paşa kurbunda Esirī Kemāl Mahallesi; Nüfūs: 190
[7] Ayasofya-yı kebīr kurbunda Molla Fenārī nām-ı diğer Hayāl Çeşme Mahallesi;
　　Nüfūs:　　　　　42

[59] Peykhāne civārında Dizdāriye Mahallesi; nüfūs: 195
[48] Eski Darbhāne kurbunda Sarrāc İshāk Mahallesi; nüfūs: 188
[48] Eski Darbhāne civārında Yakūb Ağa Mahallesi; nüfūs: 448
[59] Peykhāne civārında Tahta Minare nām-ı diğer Hamza Bey Mahallesi; nüfūs: 80
[7] Gedik Paşa civārında Divāne ʿAli Mahallesi
  Nüfūs: 384
                005 [Kazābādī [?] medreseninde sākin talebeden]
                389
[48] Eski Darbhāne civārında Soğan Ağa Mahallesi; nüfūs: 74
[61] Kumkapı dāhilinde Tavāşī Süleymān Ağa Mahallesi; nüfūs: 173
[61] Kumkapı civārında Cerrāh İshāk Bey nām-ı diğer Kazgānī Saʿdī
     Mahallesi; nüfūs: 145
[61] Kumkapı dāhilinde Dülbendci Hüsāmeddin Mahallesi; nüfūs: 106

[61] Kumkapı dāhilinde Muhsine Hatun nām-ı diğer İbrahim Paşa
     Mahallesi; nüfūs: 273
[61] Kumkapı civārında Nişancı Paşa-yı ʿAtīk Mahallesi; nüfūs: 271
[61] Kumkapı hāricinde Kürkçübaşı Süleymān Ağa Mahallesi; nüfūs: 58
[43] Koska civārında Çoban Çavuş Mahallesi; nüfūs: 161
[48] Koska kurbunda Miʿmār Kemāleddin Mahallesi
  Nüfūs: 451
                005 [Hekīm Çelebi medresesinde mevcūd talebeden]
                456
[48] Lāleli civārında Kuyumcu Bahflāyīş Mahallesi; nüfūs: 237
[48] Lāleli kurbunda Molla Kestel Mahallesi; nüfūs: 278
[48] Lāleli civārında Kızıltaş Mahallesi; nüfūs: 535
[49] Lāleli civārında Mesīh Paşa-yı ʿAtīk Mahallesi; nüfūs: 535
[48] Okçularbaşı civārında Emīn Bey Mahallesi; nüfūs: 412
[49] Lāleli kurbunda Kemāl Paşa Mahallesi; nüfūs: 442
[45] Şehzādebaşı civārında Hoşkadem Mahallesi
  Nüfūs: 400
                008 [Ankaravī Medresesinde sākin talebeden]
                408
[42] Aksarāy kurbunda Oruç Gāzi Mahallesi; nüfūs: 648
[42] Aksarāy kurbunda ʿAlem Bey Mahallesi; nüfūs: 294
[48] Aksarāy civārında Koğacı Dede Mahallesi; nüfūs: 434
[42] Aksarāy civārında Yaʿkūb Ağa Mahallesi; nüfūs: 247
[43] Aksarāy kurbunda Gurebā Hüseyin Ağa Mahallesi; nüfūs: 510
[43] Aksarāy kurbunda Horhor Çeşmesi civārında Kızıl Mināre Mahallesi; nüfūs: 224
[43] Aksarāy kurbunda Horhor Çeşmesi civārında Baba Hasan ʿAlemī Mahallesi;
  Nüfūs: 263
                007 [Bosnevī Darü'l-hadīs medresesinde sākin talebe]
                270
[43] Aksarāy civārında Baklalı Kemālleddin Mahallesi; nüfūs: 235
[62] Langa yeni kapısı kurbunda Çakır Ağa nām-ı diğer Mercimek
     Mahallesi; nüfūs: 686
[62] Langa yeni kapısı kurbunda Musallā nām mahalde Şeyh Ferhād
     Mahallesi; nüfūs: 545
[62] Langa yeni kapısı kurbunda İne Bey Mahallesi; nüfūs: 106
[62] Langa yeni kapısı civārında Kātib Kāsım Mahallesi; nüfūs: 188
[61] Kumkapı civārında Çadırcı Ahmed Çelebi nām-ı diğer Bālī Paşa
     Mahallesi; nüfūs: 304
[48] Tavşāntaşı kurbunda Kātib Sinān Mahallesi; nüfūs: 114

[7] Ayasofya-i kebīr Mahallesi el-maʿrūf; nüfūs: 552
[7] Ayasofya-i kebīr kurbunda Üskübī Mahallesi; nüfūs: 159
[7] Ayasofya-i kebīr kurbunda Yerebatan Mahallesi; nüfūs: 333
[7] Dikilitaş kurbunda Molla Fenārī Ahmed Paşa Mahallesi; nüfūs: 32

CİBʿALİ KOLU

[8] Süleymāniye kurbunda Kātib Şemseddin Mahallesi; nüfūs: 324
[53] Süleymāniye kurbunda Şeyh Ebulvefā civārında Şemşeddin Molla
Gürānī Mahallesi; Nüfūs: 499
[53] Süleymāniye Mahallesi
Nüfūs: 589
004 [Tābhāne Medresesinde sākin talebeden]
593
[52] Şeyh Ebulvefā kurbunda Sarı Bāyezīd Mahallesi; nüfūs: 272
[52] Şeyh Ebulvefā kurbunda Darü'l-hadīs Mahallesi
Nüfūs: 312
009 [Şeyh Ebulvefā medresesinde sākin talebeden]
321
[52] Şeyh Ebulvefā kurbunda Baba Hākī nām-ı diğer Yahyā Güzel Mahallesi
Nüfūs: 264
[52] Şeyh Ebulvefā kurbunda Voynuk Secāʿaddin Mahallesi; nüfūs: 186
[46] Atpazarı civārında Maânisalı Mehmed Paşa Mahallesi; nüfūs: 701
[45] Destgāhcılar civārında Ferhād Ağa Mahallesi; nüfūs: 145
[45] Destgāhcılar civārında Hüsām Bey Mahallesi
Nüfūs: 444
012 [Gazanfer Ağa medresesinde sākin talebeden]
456
[45] Kırkçeşme kurbunda Firūz Ağa Mahallesi; nüfūs: 308
[45] Kırkçeşme kurbunda İbrāhim Ağa Mahallesi; nüfūs: 370
[45] Sarāchāne civārında Miʿmār Abbas Mahallesi
Nüfūs: 730
006 [Hüseyin Paşa medresesinde sakin olan talebeden]
736
[45] Sarāchāne kurbunda Dülgerzāde Mahallesi
Nüfūs: 341
003 [Bahāriye medresesinde sākin olan talebeden]
344
[45] Koğacılar civārında Revāniciler Mahallesi; nüfūs: 48
[45] Sarāchāne civārında Haydarhān Mahallesi; nüfūs: 309
[51] Zeyrek civārında Şāh Çobān Mahallesi; nüfūs: 268
[51] Zeyrek kurbunda Kasāb Timūr Hān Mahallesi; nüfūs: 456
[51] Molla Zeyrek Mahallesi el-maʿrūf; nüfūs: 400
[51] Çırçır civārında Hācı Hasan Mahallesi
Nüfūs: 381
003 [Hācı Hasanzāde medresesinde sākin talebeden]
384
[51] Çırçır civārında Haydar Paşa Mahallesi; nüfūs: 171
[54] Kadı çeşmesi civārında Kātib Hüsrev Mahallesi; nüfūs: 163
[54] Kadı çeşmesi civārında Altıboğāça Mahallesi;
Nüfūs: 413
001 [Kıbrīsī Darü'l-hadīsi medresesinde sākin talebeden]
414

[54] Kadı çeşmesi civārında 'İmāret-i 'atīk Mahallesi;
    Nüfūs: 255
                  004 [Mu'ayyid Ahmed Efendi medresesinde sākin talebeden]
                  259
[54] Kadı çeşmesi civārında Sinān Ağa Mahallesi
    Nüfūs: 159
                  002 [Sālihzāde medresesinde sākin talebeden]
                  161
[54] Kadı çeşmesi civārında Yārhisār Mustafa Muslihiddin Mahallesi
    Nüfūs: 186
                  003 [Şerīfzāde Mehmed Ağa medresesinde sākin talebeden]
                  189
[54] Müfti Hamāmı kurbunda 'Aşık Paşa Mahallesi
    Nüfūs: 517
                  004 [Mi'mār Sinān medresesinde sākin talebeden]
                  521
[54] Haydar kurbunda Hācı Ferhād Mahallesi; nüfūs: 322
[54] Küçük Mustafa Paşa kurbunda Molla Hüsrev Mahallesi; nüfūs: 540
[54] Küçük Mustafa Paşa civārında Gül Cāmi'i Mahallesi; nüfūs: 712
[54] Cib'ali kurbunda Üsküblü Mahallesi; nüfūs: 329
[54] Cib'ali kapısı dāhilinde Seferīkoz Mahallesi; nüfūs: 309
[52] Kapān-ı dakīk kurbunda Haraccı Kara Mehmed Mahallesi; nüfūs: 499
[55] Kapān-ı dakīk kurbunda Yāvuzer Sinān Bey Mahallesi; nüfūs: 318
[55] Kapān-ı dakīk dāhilinde Papasoğlu Mahallesi; nüfūs: 42
[55] Kapān-ı dakīk kurbunda 'Azebler civārında Elvānzāde Mahallesi;
    Nüfūs: 608
[52] Kapān-ı dakīk kurbunda Hızır Bey Mahallesi; nüfūs: 1011
[55] Kapān-ı dakīk kurbunda Bıçakcı 'Alā'addīn Mahallesi; nüfūs: 247
[55] Kapān-ı dakīk kurbunda Hācı Halil 'Attār Mahallesi; nüfūs: 527
[55] Sālih Paşa kurbunda Şeyh Muhyiddīn Koçevī Mahallesi; nüfūs: 301
[55] Sālih Paşa kurbunda ‹bn-i Meddas Mahallesi; nüfūs: 501
[9] Küçük Bāyezīd kurbunda Hoca Gıyāseddīn Mahallesi; nüfūs: 426
[9] Ayāzma kapısı dāhilinde Hoca Hayreddīn Mahallesi; nüfūs: 729
[9] Odun kapısı kurbunda Sarı Demirci Mahallesi; nüfūs: 236
[9] Odun kapısı kurbunda Hoca Hamza Mahallesi; nüfūs: 329
[9] Taht al-kal'a kurbunda Timūrtaş Mahallesi; nüfūs: 79
[53] Dīvoğlu çeşmesi civārında Kepenekci Sinān Mahallesi
    Nüfūs: 119
                  004 [Kepenekçi Sinān medresesinde sākin talebeden]
                  123
[49] Vezneciler civārında Camcı 'Ali Mahallesi; nüfūs: 334
[43] Şehzade kurbunda Kalenderhāne Mahallesi
    Nüfūs: 591
                  008 [Cedīd İbrāhīm Paşa medresesinde sākin talebeden]
                  599
                  008 [Kalenderhāne medresesinde sākin talebeden]
                  607
[43] Şehzāde kurbunda Emīn Nūreddīn Mahallesi
    Nüfūs: 333
                  006 [Mahmūd Efendi [Efendi] medresesinde sākin talebeden]
                  339
                  024 [Şehzāde medresesinde sākin talebeden]
                  363

[43] Şehzāde civārında Balabān Ağa Mahallesi; nüfūs: 403
[45] Şehzāde kurbunda İbrāhīm Paşa Hamāmı civārında Muhtesib
   Karag"z Mahallesi; nüfūs: 292
[46] Sultān Mehmed kurbunda Harāccı Muhyiddīn Mahallesi
   Nüfūs: 646
                002 [Tūtī ʿAbdüllatīf medresesinde sākin talebeden]
                648
[9] Kıble çeşmesi kurbunda Suhte Hatīb Mahallesi; nüfūs: 152
[52] Şeyh Ebu'l-vefā kurbunda Molla Hüsrev Mahallesi
   Nüfūs: 1020
                0014 [Ekmekçizāde Ahmed Paşa medresesinde sākin talebeden
                005 [Hasan Ağa Dārü'l'hadīsi medresesinde sākin talebeden
                1039

BALĀT KOLU

[46] Sultān Mehmed kurbunda Şeyh Resmī Mahallesi
   Nüfūs: 246
                004 [Sultān Mehmed medreselerinden Bahr-i Siyāh tarafında Āyāk
                   Kurşunlu medresesinde sākin talebeden]
                007 [Sultān Mehmed'de medāris-i sahn- ı semānīden baş
                   medreseden]
                257
[46] Sultān Mehmed civārında Miʿmār Sinān Mahallesi
   Nüfūs: 820
                004 [Niflancı[?] Paşa medārisinden Tahtānī medresesinde sākin
                   talebeden]
                013 [Medrese-i Hāfız Paşa'da sākin talebeden]
                837
[46] Sultān Mehmed civārında Kirmāsti Mahallesi
   Nüfūs: 271
                006 [Servili medresesinde sākin talebeden]
                004 [Cedīde ʿAbdürrahīm medresesinde sākin talebeden]
                003 [Sultān Mehmed'de tetemme-i rābiʿa medresesinde sākin
                   talebeden]
                284
[27] Sultān Mehmed kurbunda Nişāncı civārında Efdalzāde Mahallesi
   Nüfūs: 115
                008 [Nişāncı-i Cedīd Çukur [?] medresesinde sākin talebeden]
                006 [Nişāncı-i [Cedīd] ? Horhor medreselerinden Fevkānī'de sākin
                   talebeden] 129
[47] Sultān Mehmed kurbunda İskender Paşa Mahallesi
   Nüfūs: 236
                015 [Sultān Mehmed medārisinden Çifte Baş Kurşunlu]
                251
[27] Sultān Mehmed civārında Çıkrıkcı Kemāleddin Mahallesi
   Nüfūs: 619
                003 [Sultān Mehmed'de Bahr-ı Sefīd tarafında Çifte Ayak
                medresesinde
                ____ sākin talebeden]
                622
[47] Küçük Karaman kurbunda Hoca Hayreddin Mahallesi

Nüfūs: 549
    004 [Velī Efendi medresesinde sākin talebeden]
    002 [Sultān Mehmed medārisinden Akdeniz tarafında Çifte Baş
    ____ medresesinde sākin talebeden]
    555

[28] Cumartesi pazarı kurbunda Mesīh Paşa nām-ı diğer Hasan Paşa Mahallesi
    Nüfūs: 225

[28] Hırka-i şerīf kurbunda Akseki Mahallesi; nüfūs: 244

[33] Sultān Mehmed kurbunda Sarıgez civārında Hasan Halīfe Mahallesi; Nüfūs: 96

[57] Kadı Çeşmesi civārında Müfti 'Ali Mahallesi; nüfūs: 364

[32] Sarıgez kurbunda Sarı Nasūh Mahallesi; nüfūs: 108

[28] Cumartesi pazarı kurbunda Molla Ahaveyn Mahallesi; nüfūs: 246

[46] Kıztaşı kurbunda Mustafa Bey Mahallesi
    Nüfūs: 174
    002 [Sultān Mehmed medārisinden Tābhāne medresesinde sākin
    talebeden]
    004 [Feyziyye Medresesinde sākin talebeden]
    180

[32] Hüsrev Paşa kurbunda Kassāb '‹vāz Mahallesi; nüfūs: 118

[32] Hüsrev Paşa kurbunda Kadı'asker Mehmed Efendi Mahallesi; nüfūs: 256

[29] Yenibağçe kurbunda Tūtī 'Abdüllatīf Mahallesi; nüfūs: 104

[29] Yenibağçe kurbunda Hürrem Çavuş Mahallesi; nüfūs: 151

[28] Yenibağçe kurbunda Akşemseddin Mahallesi; nüfūs: 334

[29] Yenibağçe kurbunda Keçeci Pīrī Mahallesi; nüfūs: 536

[29] Karagümrük kurbunda Altāy Çeşmesi civārında Debbāğzāde Elhāc Hasan
Mahallesi
    Nüfūs: 344
    005 [Cedīd 'Ali Paşa medresesinde sākin talebeden]
    349

[29] Karagümrük kurbunda Muhtesib İskender Mahallesi
    Nüfūs: 297
    003 [Sekbān 'Ali medresesinde sākin talebeden]
    300

[28] Cumartesi pazarı kurbunda Hoca Üveys Mahallesi; nüfūs: 707

[29] Yenibāğçe kurbunda Hoca Hayreddin Mahallesi; nüfūs: 89

[28] Edirne kapısı kurbunda Hādīce Sultān Mahallesi; nüfūs: 640

[26] Sultān Selīm kurbunda Mi'mār Şecā'eddīn Mahallesi
    Nüfūs: 98
    05 [Zekeriyā Evliya Medresesinde sākin talebeden]
    113

[26] Fethiye kurbunda Kātib Muslihiddīn Mahallesi
    Nüfūs: 625
    009 [Fethiye medresesinde sākin talebe]
    634

[26] Çehārşanbe pazarı kurbunda Koğacı Dede Mahallesi
    Nüfūs: 332
    001 [Debbāğzāde medresesinde sākin talebeden]
    333
    008 [Koğacı Dede medresesinde sākin talebeden]
    341

[26] Çehārşenbe pazarı kurbunda Beyceğiz Mahallesi;
    Nüfūs: 449
    007 [Mehmed Ağa Dārü'l-hadīsinde sākin talebeden]

456
[26] Sultān Selīm kurbunda Çerāğī Hamza Mahallesi
    Nüfūs: 464
              004 [Müfti Hüseyin Efendi medresesinde sākin talebeden]
              002 ['İzzet Mehmed Efendi medresesinde sākin talebeden]
              470
[27] Sultān Selīm kurbunda Cebecibaşī Mahallesi
    Nüfūs: 200
              002 [Kadı'asker Mustafa Efendi medresesinde sākin talebeden]
              006 [Es'ad Efendi medresesinde sākin talebeden]
              208
[26] Sultān Selīm kurbunda Debbāğ Yunus Mahallesi
    Nüfūs: 578
              004 [Yahyā Efendi medresesinde sākin talebeden]
              582
[27] Çehārşenbe pazarı kurbunda Tevki'i Ca'fer Mahallesi
    Nüfūs: 151
              006 [Papasoğlu medresesinde sākin talebeden]
              157
[27] Sultān Selīm civārında Hatīb Muslihiddin Mahallesi; nüfūs: 227
[27] Dırāğman kurbunda Tercümān Yunus Mahallesi; nüfūs: 590
[27] Mehmed Ağa Cāmi'i kurbunda Dervīş 'Ali Mahallesi
    Nüfūs: 545
              002 [Defterdār-ı esbak İbrāhīm Efendi medresesinde sākin talebeden]
              537
[29] Karagümrük kurbunda 'Atīk 'Ali Paşa Mahallesi
    Nüfūs: 851
              003 [Kaba Halīl Efendi medresesinde sākin talebeden]
              002 [Kāzī 'asker Hasan Efendi medresesi]
              005 ['Atīk 'Ali Paşa medresesi]
              861
[27] Edirne kapısı kurbunda Çukurbostān civārında Kāsım Ağa Mahallesi
    Nüfūs: 129
              002 [Üç baş medresesinde sākin talebeden]
              131
[29] Yenibāğçe kurbunda Mi'mār Sinān Mahallesi; nüfūs: 360
[32] Yenibāğçe kurbunda Karabaş Hüseyin Ağa Mahallesi; nüfūs: 897
[28] Edirne kapısı kurbunda Neslişāh Sultān Mahallesi
    Nüfūs: 454
              264 [Sulukule'de mütemekkin tāife-i Kıptiyān]
              718
[27] Edirne kapısı kurbunda Cāfer Ağa Mahallesi; nüfūs: 181
[27] Edirne kapısı kurbunda El-hāc Muhyiddin Mahallesi; nüfūs: 179
[11] Salma Tomruk kurbunda Kefevī Mahallesi; nüfūs: 263
[11] Salma Tomruk kurbunda Ka'riye-i 'Atīk 'Ali Paşa Mahallesi
    Nüfūs: 481
              007 [Ka'riye medresesinde sākin talebeden]
              488
[11] Kesme Kaya kurbunda Hoca Kāsım G"nānī Mahallesi; nüfūs: 378
[11] Kesme Kaya nām mahalde Hammāmī Muhyiddin Mahallesi; nüfūs: 278
[12] Eğrikapı dāhilinde Molla 'Aşkī Mahallesi; nüfūs: 461
[13] Salma Tomruk kurbunda Kemānkeş Kara Mustafa Paşa Mahallesi; nüfūs: 116
[12] Eğrikapı kurbunda Hoca 'Ali Mahallesi

Nüfūs: 114
                <u>245</u> [tāife-i Kiptiyān]
                359
[12] Eğrikapı kurbunda El-hāc İlyās Mahallesi
    Nüfūs: 415
                <u>379</u> [tāife-i Kiptiyān]
                794
[12] Eğrikapı kurbunda Avcı Bey Mahallesi; nüfūs: 416
[14] Ebu Ensārī kapısı dāhilinde Toklu Dede Mahallesi; nüfūs: 147
[14] Ebu Ensārī kapısı dāhilinde ʿAtīk Mustafa Paşa Mahallesi
    Nüfūs: 86
                <u>48</u> [tāife-i Kiptiyān]
                134
[6] Balāt kapısı dāhilinde Hızır Çavuş Mahallesi; nüfūs: 97
[6] Balāt kapısı hāricinde Karabaş Mahallesi; nüfūs: 48
[6] Balāt kapısı kurbunda El-hāc ʿİsa Mahallesi; nüfūs: 395
[17] Fener [Fenār] kapısı dāhilinde Tahta Mināre Mahallesi; nüfūs: 115
[17] Fener kapısı dāhilinde Caʿfer Subaşı Mahallesi; nüfūs:196
[17] Fener kapısı dāhilinde ʿAbdī Subaşı Mahallesi; nüfūs: 88
[55] Cibʿali Yenikapısı dāhilinde Karabaş nām-ı diğer Çukur Mahallesi
    Nüfūs: 345
[27] Sultān Mehmed kurbunda Pirinçci Sinān Mahallesi
    Nüfūs: 185
                <u>004</u> [Esseyyid Yahyā Tevfīk Efendi medresesinde sākin talebeden]
                189
[43] Aksarāy kurbunda Sūfiler Mahallesi; nüfūs: 553

TOPKAPI KOLU

[42] Aksarāy kurbunda Murād Paşa Mahallesi; nüfūs: 807
[42] Murād Paşa kurbunda Kazgānī Saʿdī Mahallesi; nüfūs: 326
[32] Sülüklü Çeşme kurbunda Sühte Sinān Mahallesi; nüfūs: 283
[42] Taş Kassāb kurbunda Sermed [Şirmet?] Çavuş Mahallesi; nüfūs: 125
[42] Taş Kassāb kurbunda Selçuk Sultān nām-ı diğerTahta Mināre Mahallesi
    Nüfūs: 268
[41] Molla Gürāni kurbunda Seydī ʿÖmer Mahallesi; nüfūs: 389
[41] Molla Gürānī kurbunda Nevbahār Mahallesi; nüfūs: 192
[41] Fenāʾī Dede kurbunda Toptaşı Mahallesi; nüfūs:96
[42] Taş Kassāb kurbunda Sarı Mūsā Mahallesi; nüfūs: 206
[32] Lütfi Paşa civārında Defterdār Ahmed Çelebi Mahallesi; nüfūs: 451
[33] Maʿcūnī Mahallesi el-maʿrūf; nüfūs: 146
[33] Maʿcūnī kurbunda Seydī Halīfe Mahallesi; nüfūs: 209
[33] Maʿcūnī kurbunda Sarı Nasūh Mahallesi; nüfūs: 113
[34] Maʿcūnī kurbunda Koruk Mahmūd Mahallesi; nüfūs: 381
[31] Şehremīni kurbunda Deniz Abdāl Mahallesi; nüfūs: 448
[31] Şehremīni civārında El-hāc Sinān Ağa Mahallesi; nüfūs: 110
[31] Şehremīni kurbunda Caʿfer Ağa Mahallesi; nüfūs: 359
[42] Molla Gürānī Mahallesi el-maʿrūf; nüfūs: 322
[33] Yaylak kurbunda El-hāc İbrāhīm Çavuş Mahallesi; nüfūs: 281
[41] Molla Gürānī kurbunda Seydī Bey Mahallesi; nüfūs: 127
[41] Molla Gürānī kurbunda El-hāc Tīmūr Mahallesi; nüfūs: 138
[42] Molla Gürānī kurbunda Nūri Dede Mahallesi; nüfūs: 271
[31] Şehzāde civārında Sarrāc Doğān Mahallesi; nüfūs: 151

[31] Şehremīni kurbunda Erikli Mahallesi; nüfūs: 415
[32] Yenibāğçe kurbunda Molla Şeref Mahallesi; nüfūs: 106
[32] Yenibāğçe kurbunda Ördek Kassāb Mahallesi; nüfūs: 382
[32] Yenibāğçe kurbunda Kapudān Sinān Paşa Mahallesi; nüfūs: 177
[41] Yenibāğçe kurbunda Molla ʿAli El-Fenārī Mahallesi; nüfūs: 148
[32] Yenibāğçe kurbunda Kātib Muslihiddin Mahallesi; nüfūs: 143
[31] Yenibāğçe kurbunda Müneccim Saʿdi Mahallesi; nüfūs: 199
[31] Yenibāğçe kurbunda Emīn-i Cev Mahallesi; nüfūs: 249
[31] Topkapı kurbunda Çivizāde Mahallesi; nüfūs: 920
[31] Topkapı kurbunda Fātma Sultān Mahallesi; nüfūs: 240
[31] Topkapı civārında İskender Ağa Mahallesi; nüfūs: 211
[31] Topkapı kurbunda Mustafa Çavuş Mahallesi; nüfūs: 85
[31] Topkapı kurbunda Kürkçübaşı Ahmed Şemseddin Mahallesi; nüfūs: 200
[31] Topkapı civārında Melek Hātūn Mahallesi; nüfūs: 142
[31] Topkapı dāhilinde Bāyezīd Ağa Mahallesi; nüfūs: 439
[33] Yeni Mevlevīhāne kapısı civārında Aydın Kethüdā Mahallesi; nüfūs: 335
[33] Mevlevīhāne Yenikapısı kurbunda El-hāc Evliyā Mahallesi; nüfūs: 277
[33] Mevlevīhāne Yenikapısı kurbunda Kātib Murād Mahallesi; nüfūs: 131
[33] Mevlevīhāne Yeni kapısı civārında Tarsūsī Mahallesi; nüfūs: 164
[33] Mevlevīhāne Yeni kapısı kurbunda Miʿmār ʿAcem Mahallesi; nüfūs: 206
[34] Silivri kapısı kurbunda Veled-i Karabaş Paşa Mahallesi; nüfūs: 298
[33] Silivri kapısı kurbunda Uzun Yūsuf Mahallesi; nüfūs: 271
[33] Silivri kapısı kurbunda Hāncı Karag"z Mahallesi; nüfūs:399
[32] Sarıgez kurbunda Öksüzce Mehmed Hatīb Mahallesi; nüfūs: 129

YEDIKULE KOLU

[38] Koca Mustafa Paşa Mahallesi el-maʿrūf
   Nüfūs: 500
                012 [Koca Mustafa Paşa medresesinde sākin talebeden]
                512
[38] Koca Mustafa Paşa kurbunda Yeldeğirmeni nām-ı diğer
ʿAli Fakih Mahallesi; nüfūs: 661
[38] Koca Mustafa Paşa kurbunda Duhāniye Mahallesi; nüfūs: 77
[38] Koca Mustafa Paşa kurbunda El-hāc Hamza Mahallesi; nüfūs: 276
[38] Koca Mustafa Paşa kurbunda Canbāziyye Mahallesi; nüfūs: 351
[41] ʿAvret pazarı kurbunda Ahmed Kethüdā Mahallesi; nüfūs: 301
[41] ʿAvret pazarı kurbunda Canbāziyye Mahallesi
   Nüfūs: 440
                007 [Cerrah Mehmed Paşa medresesinde sākin talebeden]
                447
[41] ʿAvret pazarı kurbunda Kürkçü Paşa Mahallesi; nüfūs: 782
[41] Haseki Sultān civārında Başcı El-hāc Mahmūd Mahallesi
   Nüfūs: 198
                012 [Haseki Sultān medresesinde sākin talebeden]
                210
[41] ʿAvret pazarı civārında Hobyār Mahallesi; nüfūs: 713
[41] Haseki Sultān kurbunda Kici [?] Hātūn Mahallesi
   Nüfūs: 207
                005 [Bayrām Paşa medresesinde sākin talebeden]
                212
[34] Altımermer kurbunda Kātib Muslihiddin Mahallesi; nüfūs: 323
[34] Dāvūd Paşa Mahallesi el-maʿrūf

Nüfūs: 1308
             0010 [Dāvūd Paşa medresesinde sākin talebeden]
             1318
[44] Dāvūd Paşa İskelesi kurbunda Kassāb İlyās Mahallesi
Nüfūs: 606
             005 [İbrahīm Paşa-yı Cedīd medresesinde sākin talebeden]
             611
[34] Dāvūd Paşa İskelesi civārında Sultān Bāyezīd-i Cedīd Mahallesi;
Nüfūs: 490
[41] Yūsuf Paşa Çeşmesi kurbunda Hācı Bayrām-ı Hāftānī Mahallesi;
Nüfūs: 254
[42] Aksarāy kurbunda Kātib Muslihiddin Mahallesi; nüfūs: 329
[42] Aksarāy kurbunda Çākır Ağa Mahallesi; nüfūs: 556
[44] Küçük Langa kurbunda Bostāncıbaşı ʿAbdullah Ağa Mahallesi
Nüfūs: 386
             057
             443
[37] Samātya kurbunda Hāce Hātūn Mahallesi; nüfūs: 281
[37] Samātya kurbunda Sancakdār Hayreddin Mahallesi; nüfūs: 549
[38] Koca Mustafa Paşa kurbunda ʿArabacı Bāyezīd Mahallesi; nüfūs: 382
[38] Koca Mustafa Paşa civārında El-hāc Hüsrev Mahallesi; nüfūs: 144
[36] Samātya civārında Çerāğī Hasan Mahallesi; nüfūs: 225
[36] Samātya kurbunda Hācı Hüseyin Mahallesi; nüfūs: 229
[36] Samātya kurbunda Mīrāhor Mahallesi; nüfūs: 169
[35] Yedikule kurbunda İlyās Çelebi Mahallesi; nüfūs: 92
[35] Yedikule kurbunda Emīne Hātūn nām-ı diğer
      Bacakbağı Mahallesi; nüfūs: 56
[35] Yedikule kurbunda Hācı Vahdeddin Mahallesi; nüfūs: 134
[35] Yedikule kurbunda Kürkçü başı Hācı Hüseyin Mahallesi;
Nüfūs: 125
[35] Yedikule kurbunda El-hāc Pīrī Mahallesi; nüfūs: 176
[35] Yedikule kalʿası derūnunda mevcūd hānelerde sākin ehl-i İslām;
Nüfūs: 90

Yekūn: mecmūʿ hāne ve medārisde olan ehl-i İslām; nüfūs: 92627
(Total number of Muslims in residences and theological seminaries)

Mecmūʿ hānelerde sākin bā-defter-i müfredāt tahrīr olunan bīkārān:
(Total number of bachelors recorded in the register)
    Müslim *(Muslim)*: 1823   Reʿāyā *(non-Muslim)*: 4262
    Yekūn *(total)*: 6085

Cemʿan yekūn nüfūs *(Total population)*:   98712

Hurrira bi-maʿrifeti el-fakīr ileyhi subhāne
Esseyyid Mūsā el-Kudsī
El-Kādī bi-dārüʾl-hilāfetiʾl-ʿaliyye
Gafara [Allah] lehu

Smokers in a traditional Turkish coffeehouse, late 19th century postcard (collection of Nezih Başgelen, Istanbul).

5

AN ETHNOGRAPHY OF VIRGINIA TOBACCO PRODUCTION IN TURKEY

EBRU KAYAALP

How can an agricultural crop that is produced and exchanged in a contemporary neo-liberal political economy change farmers' relationships with their nation-state? How does a crop transform the social and political settings of its growers? Which actors, other than farmers, are involved in this process and how does their presence change farmers' bonds with their crop, land, and labor?

On the basis of the preliminary fieldwork I conducted in Düzce, Turkey, during the summer of 2004 and between 2005 and 2006, I seek to answer these questions through a discussion of Virginia tobacco production. I propose that the production of Virginia tobacco, which is a direct outcome of the introduction of free market economic policies into Turkey, not only has been bringing about a new relationship between farmers and their crops, lands, and labor with the introduction of contract farming, but also has been transforming farmers' attachment to the Turkish nation-state. As the enforcer of the rules of the International Monetary Fund and the World Bank in the last two decades, Turkey has been actively cutting back the welfare benefits of its citizens. The farmers in Düzce, who are negatively affected by these policies, have sought alternatives for their livelihood. The alternatives they have chosen are working for the multinational tobacco companies to produce Virginia tobacco or initiating organic vegetable farming projects with non-governmental organizations (NGOs). In both cases, however, the farmers' actions and decisions are regulated at every step: by the laws of the government, by the standards of multinationals, by the decisions of Turkish tobacco experts, and by the procedures of the sponsors of organic farming, which, in turn, govern the farmers as subjects of neo-liberalism. David Harvey defines neo-liberalism as "a theory of political economic practices that proposes that human well-being can best be advanced by liberating individual entrepreneurial freedoms and skills within an institutional framework characterized by strong private property rights, free markets, and free trade."[1] By enforcing the intensification and expansion of free markets and liberal economic policies, neo-liberalism emerges as a mode of governing practice, which

[1] David Harvey, *A Brief History of Neoliberalism* (Oxford: Oxford University Press, 2005), 2.

constitutes individuals as responsible actors who maximize quality of life through their acts of choice, seeking to fulfill themselves within a variety of micro-domains.

This chapter has five sections: The first section discusses the economic liberalization process that Turkey has been undergoing since the 1980s. Deregulation of agricultural policies will be examined with a particular focus on the tobacco sector. In the second part, drawing on my fieldwork in Düzce, I shall present the reasons why farmers ceased the cultivation of Oriental tobacco, which had been grown in the region for generations. I will then discuss the history of Virginia tobacco production in Düzce and compare the production processes of these two types of tobacco.[2] The third section will elaborate more specifically the newly introduced system of contract farming and explain how it has changed the modes of tobacco production. In contract farming, growers produce their crops in accordance with agreements that specify the conditions of production and marketing. Here we shall also see how standards intended to bring about more transparent and efficient production function to create comparable settings in different domains. The fourth section will address the farmers' complaints about Virginia tobacco production and offer some suggestions as to why the farmers do not switch to other crops in spite of their criticisms. I will also discuss organic vegetable farming in Düzce, which aspired to become an alternative to Virginia tobacco production but failed to do so. The conclusion will demonstrate that the bond connecting the farmers to the Turkish nation-state has changed under neo-liberalism, which governs farmers through their regulated choices of autonomous agents as citizens, farmers, and entrepreneurs.

ONCE UPON A (NEO-LIBERAL) TIME IN TURKEY

The year 1980 was a turning point in Turkish history. A major program of economic stabilization was put into operation—one that had received strong external support from international agencies. The program aimed to reduce the role of government in production by increasing the involvement of market forces, which meant the replacement of an inward-oriented policy with an export-oriented strategy. The World Bank desired to showcase Turkey as a model for the rest of the world, channeling a significant amount of resources to Turkey between 1980 and 1984 in the form of five successive Structural Adjustment

---

[2]Turkey is the world's largest producer of Oriental tobacco, usually known as Turkish tobacco. Virginia tobacco, which constitutes the highest proportion in typical American-blend cigarettes, is not extensively produced in Turkey. Compared to 147,000 tons of Oriental tobacco, Turkey produces only 6,000 tons of Virginia tobacco, and of that 90 percent is grown in Düzce; State Planning Organization (DPT), *Ninth Five-Year Development Plan (2007–2013) on Tobacco and Tobacco Products* (Ankara: DPT 2006), 17.

Loans. Turkey also signed three Stand-By Agreements with the IMF. However, this new accumulation model resulted in the longest and most broadly based decline of wages and agricultural incomes in the republican period (1924–present).[3] Influential reforms in the agricultural sector started only in the mid-1990s.[4] In 1995, Turkey signed a binding document, the Agreement on Agriculture (AoA), with the World Trade Organization (WTO), which requires the removal of tariffs against imported agricultural products as well as the elimination of support policies for agriculture. In its Letter of Intent to the IMF on 9 December 1999, Turkey announced that the government would gradually eliminate its credit subsidy to farmers.

One of the agricultural sectors profoundly affected by the rapid deregulation of agriculture was tobacco production. In 1984 the Turkish government opened its markets to foreign tobacco companies as part of its effort to follow free-market policies. Although foreign companies were allowed to ship their cigarettes into the country, the state-run tobacco monopoly, Tobacco, Tobacco Products, Salt and Alcohol Enterprises (TEKEL), maintained control over pricing and distribution, which allowed domestic production to compete effectively with the cigarette imports. But by 1991, the tobacco multinationals were granted the right to produce their own cigarettes in Turkey.

In the framework of commitments made to the IMF,[5] on January 3, 2002, the Turkish Parliament ratified the *Tobacco Law* to deregulate its tobacco industry. Until then, the government supported tobacco farmers by buying the entire crop they produced each year. But the price was often set with political considerations in mind, at levels bearing no resemblance to the true market value. Turkish government officials argued that their state-subsidized system encouraged overproduction and increased the tobacco surplus in TEKEL's depots, which would be left to rot or in fact burned up. The cost of manufacturing tobacco products in Turkey had increased to a level above international market prices, thus making it uncompetitive.

The proposed *Tobacco Law* aimed to replace the price support system with one based on competitive auctions[6] and contract farming. The new law envisaged limiting the areas where tobacco could be grown, and it also mandated the

[3] Korkut Boratav, *Türkiye İktisat Tarihi 1908–2002* (İstanbul: İmge Yayınları, 1988), 135.

[4] Oğuz Oyan, "From Agricultural Policies to an Agriculture without Policies," in S. Savran, ed., *The Ravages of Neo-Liberalism* (New York: Nova, 2002).

[5] The issue of tobacco production had been raised continuously in the Letters of Intent to the IMF from 1999 to 2003.

[6] Auctioning has barely been practiced in tobacco sales in Turkey. Contract farming, however, has become the preferred system, in which TEKEL or private tobacco buyers purchase the harvests of individual farmers according to agreements indicating the quality and quantity of tobacco.

[75]

incremental privatization of TEKEL. It established a seven-person regulatory board whose members are appointed by the government.[7] The law also allowed companies that produce more than two billion cigarettes annually within Turkey to import, price, and sell more of a similar range of products. And finally, it called for the lifting of restrictions on imports of cigarettes made from Virginia tobacco, which Turkish consumers had come to prefer.

More than one million people[8] depend on tobacco for a living in Turkey, and many growers feared that this law would destroy domestic industry and deliver it into the hands of foreign companies. Turkey is the world's largest producer of Oriental tobacco and the sixth-largest producer of tobacco in general, but it has been losing its prominent status on the global market since the introduction of liberalization policies. As the number of tobacco producers dropped from 583,000 to 255,000 between the years of 2000 and 2005, the amount of tobacco produced in Turkey also declined from 208,000 tons to 147,000 tons in the same time period.[9] On the other hand, the market demand for Virginia tobacco, which is the basic ingredient of the American-blend cigarettes, has been rapidly increasing with the change in Turkish smokers' preferences from Oriental to American-blend cigarettes. Only 10 percent of the Virginia tobacco used in American-blend cigarettes is grown in Turkey, however, and the remainder is imported from other countries. Tobacco imports, of which Virginia tobacco constitutes the largest amount, rose to 66,000 tons in 2005, costing Turkey $240 million.[10]

Although Virginia tobacco was first produced in several regions of Turkey in 1938,[11] its cultivation ceased on several occasions due to the high cost of establishing flue-cured tobacco complexes, as well as unsuitable climate conditions and the Turkish consumers' preference for Oriental tobaccos. After the enactment of the law in 1991 that granted multinational tobacco companies the right to produce their cigarettes in Turkey, cultivation of Virginia tobacco began to be undertaken on a regular basis. What was brought in from the United States,

---

[7] Among the board members of this authority there are no tobacco or any other farmers. The chair of the board is a civil servant who studied management and then worked as the deputy director of TEKEL. He is neither a tobacco farmer nor an expert. Neither are the doctor, three engineers, and two economists on the board. In the hierarchy of expertise, economists usually hold the first rank in Turkey.

[8] State Planning Organization, *Ninth Five-Year Development Plan*, 13.

[9] Tobacco Products and Alcoholic Beverages Market Regulatory Authority (TAPDK), www.tapdk.gov.tr.

[10] State Planning Organization, *Ninth Five-Year Development Plan*, 37.

[11] For research studies considering Turkish production of Virginia tobacco in 1938, see Z. Akkoyunlu, K. Gültekin, and H. Pazın, "Tütün İnstitüsünün Virjinya [Flue-Cured] Tütünleri Üzerindeki 1938 Çalışması," *Tütün İnstitüsü Raporları* 2/2 (1939).

however, was not only the seeds for Virginia tobacco, but also the way to grow it—that is, contract farming. In a system controlled by the tobacco companies, contract farming has emerged as a new method of production in Turkey, changing the farmers' relationship with their crop, land, and labor.

ORIENTAL VERSUS VIRGINIA TOBACCO

Düzce is an interesting location for examining the transformation in tobacco production because it is an area where both Oriental and Virginia tobacco have been cultivated in different periods. Virginia tobacco is now the primary cash crop in this region, produced in large quantities for multinational tobacco companies, although in the past, Oriental tobacco was cultivated as the primary crop.

All the people interviewed who are currently growing Virginia tobacco had cultivated Oriental tobacco in the past. When the multinational tobacco companies entered the region, most of the farmers had already stopped growing Oriental tobacco because of the low prices paid for their crop by TEKEL.

Oriental tobacco, which involves labor-intensive farming, had not earned enough to compensate for the labor involved. Along with low prices, decisions of the experts of the state-run monopoly regarding the grade and amount of tobacco created disagreements between the officials and the farmers. Interviewees reported that large quantities of tobacco leaves were incinerated by the state officials on the grounds that they were low in quality. However, the Turkish government has always been reluctant to buy the entire amount of tobacco offered by the farmers, owing to the surplus in the stockpiles of tobacco leaves in their depots. Thus, their policy usually involved arbitrary judgments regarding the quality and amount of the tobacco leaves.

In one of my interviews, one farmer sadly recalled memories of his tobacco being burned: "We had 1,800 kilos of dried tobacco and brought the tobacco leaves to TEKEL's office. They bought only 600 kilos of it and told us to burn the rest. They had hired people to burn the tobacco leaves. These people set the leaves on fire. Then we realized that all our efforts were for nothing."

Eventually all the farmers in these villages stopped growing Oriental tobacco and switched to other crops, such as wheat and corn, neither of which was particularly lucrative. The farmers began to produce Virginia tobacco because of the restrictions in agricultural policies established by the Turkish government.

Düzce's humid climate, its strategic location between the two big cities, Ankara and Istanbul, the presence of irrigation systems in the region, and the farmers' past experience with Oriental tobacco are among the reasons the multinational tobacco companies preferred this region. Farmers hesitated at first to go into business with tobacco multinationals. One of the farmers, who had participated in one of the briefings by a multinational company in 1985, said that the company's description of Virginia tobacco production seemed different and strange to them. The Turkish farmers were told how to grow tobacco in a more 'scientific' way. In the end, company representatives offered a set amount (equal to $386 per decare—1,000 square meters) for each farmer who would be assigned to the multinational tobacco company. After being offered a guaranteed payment, with or without any crop in return, many farmers agreed to work for the multinational company. After the first year, the farmers were rewarded with an extra bonus. The entrance of another multinational tobacco company in 1993 increased the number of farmers and of lands allocated to Virginia tobacco planting.

The techniques of Virginia tobacco production are totally different from those of Oriental tobacco, which requires "more work but brings less money in the end." Oriental tobacco farming has a production cycle of one year. It requires fertilization with manure, and no irrigation is needed other than rain. All the leaves are picked at once and sun-cured. The dried leaves are baled and brought to the offices of TEKEL for payment.

Virginia tobacco production has a 10-month production cycle, and a high quantity of fertilizers and pesticides are used. The seeds, which are supplied by the companies, are grown in Styrofoam boxes,[12] then placed in concrete pools constructed by the farmers. Irrigation of the soil is required after each five or six sessions of plucking tobacco plant leaves. Tobacco leaves are taken to the ovens of multinational companies for curing. The companies pay the farmers according to a contract signed at the beginning of the crop cycle.

CROP, LAND, LABOR ASSEMBLAGES

Contract farming has dramatically changed the relations between farmers and their crops, lands, and labor in Düzce.

Crop

Even though it is not explicitly stated in the contract signed between farmers and multinationals, the crop is considered to be the possession of the multinational companies even before the farmer "sells" it to the companies.

Dated April 2, 2003 the contract states: "The farmer cannot sow and produce

---

[12] Styrofoam was first used in tobacco production in Turkey after the use of methyl bromide in soil was prohibited by the Turkish government in 2004. In the float system, usually practiced in greenhouses, the first step is to construct a cement container and fill it with a nutrient solution. Pesticides are also added to the solution. Styrofoam trays are filled with a soil-less medium (vermiculite, perlite, and peat moss) and seeded with pelletized seeds, which float on the solution. After a couple of months, when the seeds sprout into seedlings, they are transferred to fields.

tobacco for another person and/or persons other than … the company as long as this contract is effective." And "after signing the contract, if the farmer decides not to grow Virginia tobacco, and/or transfers his right to produce tobacco to another person, he is obliged to return all inputs supplied by the company [such as seeds, fertilizers, pesticides, equipments, etc.] and to pay back three times the value of the total sum of the services provided by the company."

As specified by the contract, "the farmers can only use the seeds supplied by the companies." This new agricultural system has led to the separation of the farmer from the production of the seed and loss of control over his own soil. As Jack Kloppenburg argues, "[t]he seed … becomes the nexus of control over the determination and shape of the entire crop production process."[13] In Oriental tobacco production, on the other hand, farmers used to grow seeds for the following year along with tobacco leaves for selling in the market.

Land

Virginia tobacco planting in Düzce has brought a new arrangement in planting the land. The increased demand for tobacco cultivation resulted in a new mode of land distribution among the farmers. Virginia tobacco can be cultivated in the same soil in a three-year rotation: that is, only after a two-year break, which has triggered the widespread rental of lands among the farmers.

The land in which tobacco has not been grown for the preceding one or two years is put into the rental market. The exchange of lands among the farmers has raised the question of the 'value' of the field. The 'past history' of the each field is disseminated among the farmers in the forms of rumors, produced and distorted by others' memories, which in the end becomes the ultimate determinant for the price anticipated.

One of the farmers explained that he rented a field for 140,000,000 TL ($100) per decare for tobacco farming that could be rented for about 30,000,000 to 40,000,000 TL ($21 to 28) for growing wheat or corn instead of Virginia tobacco. The land in which tobacco has not been cultivated in the last two years is the most valuable, and there is a huge competition for it. The negotiations for and transfers of land among the farmers are carried out on an interpersonal level rather than in public meetings open to everyone. Hence, undertaking the necessary steps in the right moments requires individual entrepreneurship and good social relations. As one of the farmers stated, "You have to get along with everybody, even with the ones you don't like."

Not only the relations among people but also the selection of other crops are determined according to the requirements of Virginia tobacco farming. Future

[13] Jack R. Kloppenburg, *First the Seed: The Political Economy of Plan Biotechnology, 1492–2000* (New York: Cambridge University Press, 1988), 201.

plans about tobacco planting have led farmers to make strategic decisions about the choice of crops to be grown in certain lands. In the words of Bruno Latour, tobacco becomes an *actant*, which has an agency that transforms the social structure.[14] According to Latour, not only humans but also things (such as microbes and commodities) are actors changing the society. Correspondingly, Virginia tobacco emerges as the main determinant according to which all farming decisions are taken in Düzce. The choice of other crops that will be cultivated for certain fields; the rental prices of lands for different crops; the social relations among farmers; the initiation of different projects in the village (which will be discussed at the end of this chapter) are decided according to the system of Virginia tobacco production. The arrangement in Düzce seems like the game of checkers, in which the first turn is played by Virginia tobacco and then the rest of the game is played in accordance with that move.

Labor

As explicitly put forward in the contracts, tobacco farming must be done under the supervision of the experts of multinationals. "Every grower undertakes the cultivation of his own seedling in his own field under the control of company's staff," and "the farmer accepts to undertake the field preparation, sowing the seedlings, fertilization, irrigation, usage of pesticides, harvesting according to the orders given by the company's staff under the control of company." Both of the two multinational tobacco companies in the region have been employing *çavuşlar*, or foremen, to supervise and control the farmers' tobacco production in the fields. I was told that most of the foremen are selected from among the farmers who planted Virginia tobacco in the past. *Çavuşlar* are the intermediaries between the companies and farmers in coordinating tobacco production. Their authority to decide who would cultivate tobacco in the next year gives them a considerable power over the farmers. An ex-*çavuş* explained his duties as follows:

> What are the duties of *çavuşlar*? [For example] I tell the peasants that I am going to sow the field 3 days later and ask them to prepare the field for planting. I tell them to water the field at 6:00 a.m. and stop watering at sunset. I tell them to hoe the soil if it needs to be. The peasant cannot decide what he is going to do. The tobacco leaves should be plucked if the *çavuş* says so. If the peasant does not obey, his name is removed from the list [of the company] and this is called to 'cross out with a red pen.' All decisions are taken by *çavuşlar*.

The disciplining of the labor of the farmers in Düzce is done under the supervision and surveillance of the *çavuşlar*, which might serve as an illustrative exam-

[14] Bruno Latour, *Science in Action: How to Follow Scientists and Engineers Through Society* (Philadelphia, PA: Open University Press, 1987), 84.

ple of Michel Foucault's *Discipline and Punish*.[15] The body is treated as a machine under disciplinary power, as Foucault argues, which involves infinitesimal surveillances, permanent controls, meticulous ordering of space. Discipline 'makes' individuals through a specific technique of power which functions as a calculated, but permanent economy.[16] In other words, discipline is founded on meticulous observation of details for purposes of control and efficient use. Contracts, which observe the standard rules of the companies in every country, aim to shape, regulate, and discipline the production and labor process of the farmer. Standardization makes strong claims to efficacy through the deployment of disciplinary power to turn the people into governable, calculating, self-regulating selves.

STANDARDIZATION OF TOBACCO, FARMER, AND COMPANY

Michael Watts observes that crops "under contract are linked to the demanding 'grade' and 'quality' standards, such as color, odor, shape, absence of blemish and they are "rigorously classified, differentiated and priced in the contract."[17] This often requires a detailed explanation of farming in the contract, such as land preparation, sowing dates, input application, timing of operations, imposition of standards and quality control.

Standards define specific products and order them in a hierarchy. Experts are assigned to decide the quality and quantity of products. The tobacco is graded and so are its producers. The systems of standardization also categorize the farmers according to their performances. Companies hire the ones who obey the rules and marginalize the ones who do not—as illustrated in the case of crossing out the names of the farmers who do not comply with the rules of the tobacco companies. According to Elizabeth Dunn, standardization does not homogenize persons, as it claims.[18] Instead, it creates inequalities among the individuals, pushing some outside the system while providing others new opportunities.

Standards require not only the qualities of the finished product and producer but also the manufacturing process itself. One of the farmers in Düzce explained

[15] Michel Foucault, *Discipline and Punish* (New York: Vintage, 1995).

[16] Ibid, 170.

[17] Michael J. Watts, "Life under Contract: Contract Farming, Agrarian Restructuring, and Flexible Accumulation," in P. D. Little and M. Watts, eds., *Living under Contract: Contract Farming and Agrarian Transformation in Sub-Saharan Africa* (Madison, WI: University of Wisconsin Press, 1994), 44.

[18] Elizabeth C. Dunn, "Standards and Person-Making in East Central Europe," in A. Ong and S. J. Collier, eds., *Global Assemblages: Technology, Politics, and Ethics as Anthropological Problems* (Oxford: Blackwell, 2005).

to me how he was unable to grow a good quantity crop a few years ago because his çavuş forced him to obey his orders, which were obviously wrong. The farmer's field, having a slope, was flooded in spite of all his warnings: "I know my field better than him ... He does not know my soil. But he is also the one who has to obey the orders. He is told that the soil should be irrigated and he makes us irrigate it ... They always apply the same methods [to every field] but you have to take into consideration the nature of your own field."

Within this system, farmers are not allowed to make independent decisions about their own fields. Their local knowledge and experience are ignored and undermined through the 'standardization' principles imposed by multinational companies. The underlying assumption is that the standards would yield the same results in different countries. One of the international experts of a multi-national company complained to me that the executives of the company were expecting the production of the same good quality tobacco leaves in every coun-try. However, although the tobacco companies have strictly applied the stan-dards, the quality of tobacco leaves varies in different countries. The expert told me grouchily that he was not able to convince the executives that there is a fact called "climate," which cannot be controlled and standardized. The idea of applying the standards in every context does not consider the fact that every country might have different configurations.

As Dunn argues, standards function as what Latour calls "immutable mobiles."[19] They are the objects, which are transferred from one community to another, having profound transformative effects without being transformed themselves. They can be "decontextualized and recontextualized, abstracted, transported, and reterritorialized, and are designed to produce functionally com-parable results in disparate domains."[20] Standards are transferred from one place to another and applied in different economic and social contexts. They are not bound by space and their efficiency derives from their applicability by different people in different locations. They not only work as tools to create comparable settings but also make it possible for multinationals to *govern at a distance*.[21]

Standards produce a homogenous space, which cuts across geographical and social divisions. Andrew Barry calls these spaces technozones, which are not structures, territories or regions but discontinuous spaces of circulation and reg-

[19] Latour, *Science in Action*.

[20] Aihwa Ong and Stephen J. Collier, "Global Assemblages, Anthropological Problems," in A. Ong and S. J. Collier, eds., *Global Assemblages: Technology, Politics, and Ethics as Anthro-pological Problems* (Oxford: Blackwell, 2005), 11.

[21] "To govern at a distance" describes "indirect mechanisms of rule" of neo-liberalism, such as the standardization of systems; see Peter Miller and Nikolas Rose, "Governing Economic Life," *Economy and Society* 19/1 (1990): 8.

ulation, and these zones are also *governed at a distance* through the instrumentalization of a regulated autonomy.[22] The tobacco complexes of multinational companies are truly technozones in that sense. Not only the machines but also the architecture of the complex and the structure of production are standardized in every country. Tobacco production is controlled and regulated in each technozone, which has its own autonomy. The international tobacco experts, who pass between different technozones, connect them to each other by providing the flow of information. They translate one technozone to another and compare them with the macro-perspective they have attained.

COMPLAINTS AND ALTERNATIVES

The farming of Virginia tobacco has brought about new models and techniques of production in Düzce. Compared to Oriental tobacco production, in which the farmers have clear-cut sovereignty over their soil, Virginia tobacco has made the farmers dependent on the knowledge, seeds, fertilizers, and pesticides provided by multinational companies. This new system of relations transferred the farmers' full authority over their territory to the *çavuşlar*, who in turn is acting on behalf of multinational companies. However, this argument does not mean that the farmers were autonomous in their decisions before multinational companies came to Düzce. There have always been constraints influencing their decisions, such as government policies, market conditions, and international agreements. Nevertheless, a farmer's choice about what and how to grow on his field—a strategic decision considering the national and international markets— is different from growing a crop following the orders of an authority.

Encountering the high demand by farmers to produce Virginia tobacco, the multinational tobacco companies gained the upper hand in selecting the farmers who would work for their companies. All the farmers I interviewed complained about the conditions of Virginia tobacco production for several reasons. The most frequently expressed complaint was about the money paid to them for their crop. Even though different prices for different grades of tobacco leaves are written in the contracts, the final money given to the farmer is determined according to the quality of tobacco leaves. Tobacco experts employed by the multinational tobacco companies grade the tobacco leaves, and claims that their expertise is favoring the companies lead to severe disputes. Most of the disagreements are resolved with farmers' full acceptance of 'expert' decisions on the grade and weight of leaves. Another basic complaint concerned the competence of the staff hired by the companies. Several farmers lamented that in many past instances their leaves were over-dried or burnt in the ovens due to the negli-

[22] Andrew Barry, *Political Machines: Governing a Technological Society* (London: Athlone, 2001), 41.

gence of the company workers, but in the end, the farmers are held liable for possible losses, and as a result they were underpaid or not paid at all.

Other than these issues, the most recurring criticisms about Virginia tobacco production are generally related to the supposed health problems involved. Almost everyone talked about the rising number of cancer cases in their villages, particularly among the women, who are usually the ones applying pesticides and other chemicals. Although there is no direct proof that the increase in cancer rates is due only to the high usage of chemicals in tobacco cultivation, all the locals accept it as a fact.

Another complaint is about the rising infertility of the fields. I was told that Virginia tobacco plants grown in the 1990s were normally about 1.5 meters tall, but they are getting smaller every year. Farmers also mentioned the weeds growing in their lands, of varieties they had never seen before planting Virginia tobacco. The farmers once raised these complaints at an official level to the head of Düzce Agriculture Association. I was told that their petition against the tobacco companies in 2002 failed to produce any response, let alone any action along with their demands, but instead brought about the crossing out of their names as well as those of their relatives from the companies' list.

In spite of their complaints concerning the conditions of growing Virginia tobacco, the farmers stated that they would continue to grow it as long as the companies stay in the region because the production of Virginia tobacco is the only way to earn a proper living. As one of the farmers put it, "Before Virginia tobacco, we did not have anything. We have got everything [through the production of Virginia tobacco]. I built my house; I bought my tractor; I got my children married. I did all these with the money I earned from Virginia tobacco production."

Farmers in this region are not allowed to produce other lucrative crops, such as sugar beets and hazelnuts, because of the quota system recently put into operation by the Turkish government. In 2000 several farmers initiated organic vegetable farming in the region as an alternative to Virginia tobacco. This project, which started with great hopes, failed after two years because of the lack of a market for the organic products within Turkey. Oriental tobacco, on the other hand, is not well remunerated and too risky to grow, since there is no guarantee that the state monopoly, now undergoing privatization, will buy the crops. In contrast, multinational tobacco companies not only guarantee to buy farmers' produce with the agreements signed every year, but they also pay a relatively large amount of money for tobacco compared to what might be earned from other crops. Because of the instability of the local markets created by the policies of the government, the farmers prefer to grow crops that have a ready market, from which they can make money for a living. In spite of the problems of contract farming, the farmers made it clear that they will continue to grow Virginia tobacco. By doing so, they manage the risks associated with the instabilities of the local market by exchanging its uncertainties for a different set of risks.

CASH WITHOUT CROP

A group of Düzce farmers initiated an organic farming project in 2000 as an alternative to Virginia tobacco production. My key collaborator, who has been in charge of the organization of organic farming in the region, explained that a cooperative was established to stabilize and sustain ecological farming among the peasants. The first organic farming was financed by certain nongovernmental organizations (NGOs), which came to Düzce to help residents recover after the damages of the two earthquakes that occurred in the region in 1999. The disastrous August 17th earthquake was followed by another devastating quake on November 12th. Ninety-five percent of Düzce was destroyed, and the town became uninhabitable.

ACT (Action by Churches Together), ECHO (European Commission Humanitarian Office), and OCHA (United Nations Office for the Coordination of Humanitarian Affairs) are among the many NGOs that provided aid to the earthquake victims in the region. Even four years after the earthquakes, 47 civil society organizations were still operating in Düzce, an exceptionally high number for Turkey.

Farmers from 18 villages cultivated more than 10,000 decares of organic crops in 2000. The story of this project was published in the newspapers and magazines, especially in the leftist ones, which celebrated the farmers as the enemies of 'imperialism.' Although the farmers in this project had a variety of ideological positions, they were represented as a homogenous group standing up to the multinational tobacco companies in Düzce. While some of the farmers seemed to be indifferent to the supposedly 'anti-imperialist' dimension of organic farming, others had internalized the discourse portrayed by the leftist magazines. For example, a respectful leader of a religious sect in the village defined organic farming as a rebellion against the multinationals: "If we cultivated Virginia tobacco, we would be working like slaves for the multinational companies."

The leaders of an organic farming project visited Tunceli, a city known as a Kurdish enclave in eastern Turkey, to inform and educate other farmers about organic farming with an aim to create a discourse of "solidarity among the farmers in Turkey." The choice of Tunceli is not coincidental given the fact that one of the non-farmer coordinators who had located international sponsors for the project was a Kurd from Tunceli. The ideological stance of this person was clearly reflected in the way in which the entire project was presented as an option that would bring an end to the suppression of the farmers by the global powers.

Not only the national but also the international movement of the farmers has become possible through this project. Some of the farmers in the project were sent to Kosovo, Skopje, and Athens with funds provided by another project, the Marmara Earthquake Rehabilitation Program (MERP), which is sponsored by the European Community. Having the opportunity to meet with other farmers and discuss the problems they encountered in the process of production, the Turkish farmers were able to adopt a broader view about organic farming and become aware of organic farming projects in different countries.

Nevertheless, the farmers' organic farming project failed at the end of its second year because of the lack of a market for organic goods within Turkey. The farmers blamed the failure on the unsupportive attitude of the government. The Turkish government, by phasing out all domestic support offered to the farmers under the policies imposed by the IMF and the World Bank, was unable to take an initiative to create a market for organic goods. The organic vegetables produced by the farmers with the funds of NGOs perished in the end because of the absence of a market. The cooperative managed to sell a certain amount of organic goods through the enterprise of several farmers, who became salesmen as well as farmers.

If money was earned during this attempt at organic farming, it was actually from the funds provided by the NGOs. Although a certain percentage of the funds melted away as they were transferred from organizations to the farmers, into local civic organizations and government bureaucracies, the farmers still received more money than they had expected. In that sense, organic farming brought in some cash without producing any crop. Realizing that farming is only one part of the agricultural sector and not even the most lucrative, Düzce farmers have started to pay attention to the funds offered for agricultural projects by various NGOs.

Two years after their failure, some farmers still insist upon organic farming, emphasizing the contrasts between Virginia tobacco and organic farming. In the opinion of these farmers, organic farming, which symbolizes independence, purity and anti-imperialism, stands out against Virginia tobacco, which signifies dependency, contamination, and imperialism. The farmers' reaction to the multinational tobacco companies, however, does not indicate an opposition to nongovernmental and supranational organizations. On the contrary, farmers, who are well informed about the details of the rules and procedures of these organizations, consider these as crucial sources to finance their projects.

Almost everyone in the village expressed a desire to grow organic crops—that is, if there were a stable market for their produce. Being aware of the incapability of the Turkish government to guarantee a market, the farmers have been exploring other ways to support their project and developing strategies to bypass Turkish bureaucracy as well as other local intermediaries between them and the NGOs. The most prominent leader of the organic farming project told me how they willingly collaborated with a very powerful politician, who is the equivalent of a mafia chief in the region, to control the funds that might come from the NGOs and to facilitate the functioning of Turkish bureaucracy. Since the Turkish government is no longer seen as trustworthy and competent, the farmers look for other solutions and agents who might help realize their project.

THE NATION-STATE

Whether in Virginia tobacco production or organic vegetable farming, the farmers in Düzce are not willing to work and collaborate with the Turkish government. The impetus behind this deliberate choice is very clear: First, by phasing out domestic support to the farmers and restricting the cultivation of certain crops in several regions of Turkey, the government has not provided options for the farmers to earn a proper living. As outlined in the previous pages, the government's quota system has already led the farmers of Düzce to work for the multinational tobacco companies in spite of their complaints. In the case of organic farming, which is said to stand as an alternative to the Virginia tobacco production in the region, the funding was entirely received from international organizations. When support was needed for the marketing of the crops and the supply of certain equipment, the government did not provide it. If Virginia tobacco farming began because of the absence of lucrative options, organic vegetable farming emerged as a prospective alternative to tobacco growing. However, each option has its own set of problems, about which the farmers remonstrate. The target of their complaints is always the Turkish nation-state, which is not able to provide the required conditions for the welfare of its citizens under the policies of neo-liberalism. Interaction with the state as the hegemonic form of power no longer makes sense, and the dominant mode of discourse has changed into one that emphasizes the relations with international actors.

If the first rationale for farmers bypassing the Turkish nation-state can be explained by the latter's incompetence, the second reason is the farmers' realization of new opportunities in the global market. In spite of their continuous complaints about tobacco farming, all of the growers acknowledge that Virginia tobacco production has definitely improved their standard of living. Likewise, the organic farming experience showed the farmers that there are agricultural options other than farming. These new opportunities have become possible with globalization, which paved the way to the intervention of international actors in local settings.

It would appear that the Turkish nation-state is becoming the transmitter and the enforcer of the rules of the IMF and the World Bank at the expense of its own citizenry. The government is actively diminishing the welfare of its own citizens. Neo-liberalism has undermined the bases of social citizenship by either decreasing or privatizing social services. Under advanced liberal rule, "individuals are seeking to *fulfill themselves* within a variety of micro-moral domains or 'communities.'"[23]

Neo-liberalism does not attempt to govern new populations by overt coercion, but instead it governs through its regulation of the choices of individual members of society. Individuals seek to "enterprise themselves," to maximize their quality of life through acts of calculative decision.[24] The farmers in Düzce, who were left stranded by the Turkish nation-state, have chosen to work for the multinational tobacco companies or initiate their own agricultural projects. They are construed as subjects of choices and aspirations, but in fact they have been making their decisions under restricted and regulated alternatives. Each path they might have chosen is regulated at every step on their way to self-fulfillment: by the laws of the government, the standards of multinationals, the decisions of tobacco experts, and the procedures of organic farming sponsors. Each of these forces—with their regulations, codes, and laws—governs the farmers through their choices.

The subjectivities of farmers in Düzce are built in a radically different way than they were formerly constituted in the course of the traditional nation-building process. They have been developing new systems of relationship with the nation-state, which can neither be defined in terms of cosmopolitanism nor of loyal citizenship. Düzce is a good example of the creation of a new category of citizen-subjects, whose bonds with international actors, either multinationals or nongovernmental organizations, are becoming stronger and more determinant than those with the Turkish nation-state. This new attachment to international organs brings about the emergence of a new kind of subjectivity that is governed by the rules of neo-liberalism.*

---

[23] Nikolas Rose, "Governing 'Advanced' Liberal Democracies," in A. Barry, T. Osborne, and N. Rose, eds., *Foucault and Political Reason: Liberalism, Neo-liberalism and Rationalities of Government* (Chicago, IL: University of Chicago Press, 1996), 57.

[24] Ibid.

*This chapter grew out of research that I have been conducting for my doctoral dissertation, and I would like to thank the following institutions whose support made that research possible: Social Science Research Council for Applied Economics Program, 2004, and the John Freely Fellowship from the American Research Institute in Turkey, 2005–2006.

CONTRIBUTORS

EMINE FETVACİ received her Ph.D. in the History of Art and Architecture from Harvard University in 2005. Her dissertation, "Viziers to Eunuchs: Transitions in Ottoman Manuscript Patronage, 1566–1617," provides a re-evaluation of the most prolific period in Ottoman manuscript production through a study of the networks of political and artistic patronage at the Ottoman court. She was awarded a Freely Fellowship in 2006–2007 for a project entitled "Multiple Visions: Official and Unofficial Illustrated Ottoman Histories." Focusing on a group of illustrated *gazaname* ("book of war") manuscripts in conjunction with writings produced by the court historian at the end of the 16th century, she considers the ways in which text and image come together in Ottoman illustrated manuscripts to represent multiple points of view. Her chapter in this volume on the office of the *şehnameci*, or court historian, grows out of this larger study. She argues that the office was not rigidly defined, and thus the illustrated manuscripts of the Ottoman court were collaborative constructs involving shifting combinations of patrons, authors, painters, and scribes. Dr. Fetvacı is currently Humanities Fellow at Stanford University.

EBRU TURAN received her Ph.D. in Near Eastern Languages and Civilizations at the University of Chicago in 2007. Her dissertation, "Ibrahim Paşa (1520–1536): A Transformation in Ottoman Kingship," follows the career of the most famous grand vizier to serve under the Ottoman Sultan Süleyman. Turan focuses on the first two decades of Süleyman's reign, when his favorite vizier Ibrahim Paşa ruled with power equal to the sultan's. Using narrative and archival sources she traces how the dual kingship may have set the stage for the bureaucratization of the Ottoman Empire that followed. Her Ph.D. research was supported by a Freely Fellowship in 2002–2003. Growing out of that study, her chapter in this volume investigates the expressions of dissent in the period of Süleyman. She suggests that because of the newly exalted status of the sultanate, Süleyman could not be criticized directly, and thus dissent was directed instead toward the grand vizier. Ibrahim Paşa had been Süleyman's slave and childhood companion, and as grand vizier with unlimited power, he became in effect the sultan's alter ego. Dr. Turan is currently Assistant Professor in the History Department at Fordham University.

CENGIZ SISMAN received his Ph.D. in History and Middle Eastern Studies at Harvard University in 2005. He received a Freely Fellowship in 2004–2005 to assist with the research for his dissertation, "A Jewish Messiah in the Ottoman

Court: Sabbatai Sevi and Emergence of the Messianic Judeo-Islamic Community in the Seventeenth-Century Ottoman Empire." Using archival sources, he documented the communal life of the messianic community and its interaction of the kabbala and Sufism during the late Ottoman Empire. A fascinating episode in Ottoman religious and cultural history, "The Lost Messiah" was the subject of a book by John Freely (2004). In the chapter in this volume, Sisman explores the perception of the communities of the followers of Sabbatai Sevi after his conversion to Islam through the various names applied to the group and its sub-sects. Sisman currently teaches in the Türkiye Odalar ve Borsalar Birliği Ekonomi ve Teknoloji Üniversitesi (TOBB-ETÜ), Ankara, Turkey.

BETÜL BAŞARAN received her Ph.D. from the Department of Near Eastern Languages and Civilizations at the University of Chicago. She was awarded a Freely Fellowship in 2003–2004 to support the research leading to her dissertation, "Remaking the Gate of Felicity: Migration, Social Control, and Policing in 18th-Century Istanbul, 1730–1789." Using police and court records in the Ottoman archives to trace a transformation in the fabric of Istanbul society and in the relation of the city and its government, her study focused on the government's efforts to maintain public order by regulating migration and public assemblies. The chapter here grows out of her archival research concerning the estimates of the population of late Ottoman Istanbul, as may be determined based on the census of 1829. Başaran currently serves as Lecturer in Islamic Studies in the Department of Philosophy and Religious Studies at the University of Chicago.

EBRU KAYAALP is a doctoral candidate in the Department of Anthropology at Rice University, with a dissertation tentatively titled "From Seed to Smoke: An Ethnography of Tobacco Production in Turkey." In an ethnographic investigation of the process of agricultural transition in Turkey, she explores how local tobacco farmers in Turkey are influenced by the recent escalation of market liberalization policies. As rapid deregulation of the Turkish economy in the 1990s affected the production of tobacco, changes in the global and local markets and trade practices transformed the lives of tobacco farmers and tobacco production in Turkey. Kayaalp's dissertation research was supported by a Freely Fellowship in 2005–2006. In her chapter in this volume she examines the impact and unintended consequences of the shift to the production of Virginia tobacco in the area of Düzce, where farmers grow tobacco for the state monopoly. Kayaalp is now completing her dissertation as a Social Science Research Council International Dissertation Fellow.

INDEX

'Abdü'l-Müteal, Sa'di bin, 33
ACT. *See* Action by Churches Together
actant. See under tobacco, Virginia
Action by Churches Together (ACT), 85
Agreement on Agriculture (AoA), 75
Ahmed Paşa: 32, 44; as İbrahim Paşa's
  rival, 26, 28; revolt in Egypt, 26–28, 31
Âli, Mustafa, 10, 18, 21
AoA. *See* Agreement on Agriculture
Arifi (Fethullah), 13–14
Avdeti (avdet): 37; connotations associated
  with, 45–46, 51; dictionary definitions
  of, 43–44; foreign observers and, 43;
  origins of, 45; translation of, 45, 46; use
  of, 42, 44–46

bailo, 29
Barry, Andrew, 82
Boğaziçi University. *See* Robert College

Çağman, Filiz, 13
Carlebach, Elisheva, 38
çavuşlar (çavuş), 80, 82–83
Celalzade Mustafa: account of Ahmed
  Paşa's revolt in Egypt, 27–29; account
  of İbrahim Paşa's appointment to
  grand vizierate, 26–27; justification of
  İbrahim Paşa's appointment to grand
  vizierate, 28, 33
census in Istanbul: 1830–31, 55; 1829,
  55–56
chief architect, in comparison with court
  historian, 14–15
cigarettes, American–blend, 76
contract farming. *See* farming, contract
corps of artisans (corps of artists), 11–13,
  15
crops: organic (*see* farming, organic); Oriental tobacco (*see* tobacco, Oriental);
  and Turkish government, 75, 87; Virginia tobacco (*see* tobacco, Virginia)

defterdar, 13, 21
Discipline and Punish (Foucault), 81
Dönme (———): connotations associated

with, 41, 43, 45, 47, 51; foreign
  observers and, 38, 43, 46–48; Ottoman
  dictionary definitions of 42–44; origins
  of, 41–42; translation of, 37, 41, 43, 45;
  use of, 37–38, 41–42, 45–46
Düzce, Turkey, 73–74, 77–81, 83–88

ECHO. *See* European Commission
  Humanitarian Office
Efendi, Ahmed Lütfi, 55–56
Efendi, Aziz Mehmed. *See Sevi, Sabbatai*
European Commission Humanitarian
  Office (ECHO), 85

farmers, Turkish: and autonomy, 73–74,
  82–83; and complaints of, 74, 82–84;
  and contract farming (*see under* farming, contract); and organic vegetable,
  74, 84–87; and relationship with crops,
  land, and/or labor, 73, 77–80; and relations with Turkish government, 73–74,
  86–88; and standardization, 81
farming (*see also* farming, organic and
  farming, contract): tobacco (*see*
  tobacco, Virginia and tobacco, Oriental); and tobacco companies (*see*
  tobacco companies, multinational)
farming, contract: and effect on crops, 74,
  77–79; and effect on farmers, 73–74,
  77–78; and effect on labor 77–81, and
  effect on land, 77–80; and standardization, 81; and Virginia tobacco (*see*
  under tobacco, Virginia)
farming, organic, 73–74, 84–88
Firdawsi: 7, 16; *Shahnama*, 7, 16–17
Ferhad Paşa, 28, 31–32
Foucault, Michel: 81; *Discipline and Punish*, 81
Freely, John: and Istanbul; and stories; and
  fellowship (*see* John Freely Fellowship)

globalization, 87

Habsburg, Charles, 29, 32
History of Sultan Süleyman (Lokman),
  15–16
Hükmi, Hasan, 15, 20

[91]

Set in Minion types
Designed by Jerry Kelly